NATIVE

ecology after settlement

CODHILL
PRESS

NATIVE

ecology after settlement

POEMS BY

NATHAN MANLEY

CODHILL PRESS

NEW YORK · NEW PALTZ

CODHILL
PRESS

codhill.com

Published in the United States of America
Library of Congress Control Number: 2024944465

ISBN 978-1-949933-28-4

Cover and Book Design by Lorna Leighton
flytedesign. · flytedesign.net

CONTENTS

Cabbage White Butterfly — 1

Plains Cottonwood — 3

Deermouse — 9

Army Cutworm (Miller) Moth — 10

Mule Deer — 11

Great Blue Heron — 12

Blue-Green Algae — 13

Rainbow Trout — 14

Ute Lady's Tresses — 15

Woodhouse's Toad — 16

Short-Eared Owl — 17

Sugar Beet — 18

Coyote — 20

Grey Garden Slug — 21

Ergot/Western Wheatgrass — 22

Indian Paintbrush — 26

Harvester Ant — 27

Pronghorn — 28

Russian Olive — 29

Canada Goose — 30

Rocky Mountain Capshell Snail — 31

Quaking Aspen/Orange Cap Bolete — 32

Powderhorn Cup Lichen — 35

Tiger Muskie — 36

Red-Railed Hawk — 38

Sagebrush — 39

Common Milkweed Bug — 40

False Parasol   42

Ponderosa Pine   43

Black-Billed Magpie   45

Black-Tailed Prairie Dog   46

Western Painted Turtle   48

Hoary Bat   49

Western Kingbird   50

Greenspire Linden   51

Rusty Crayfish & Northern Crayfish   52

Dandelion   54

Urban Fox   55

Cocklebur   56

Soapweed Yucca   57

Mallard   58

Bridge Spider   59

Rocky Mountain Elk   60

Herring Gull   61

Garter Snake   63

Yellow-Barred Tiger Salamander   64

Colorado Hairstreak Butterfly/Gambel Oak   65

Mountain Plover   66

Rocky Mountain Bighorn Sheep   67

Index of Species Identifications   69

Bibliography   75

Acknowledgements   79

To what remains

The lava cools,

The blue ice comes and goes

The forests rise and wander,

The boys spin their wooden tops, the finches sing,

But never a maple cries to be young again,

Nor sediment of river turns to stone

With lamentation: It should be otherwise...

— *Thomas Hornsby Ferril, "The Long Dimension"*

Cabbage White Butterfly

Pieris rapae

> *It was observed that immediately after the insects*
> *had been killed through the application of high*
> *frequency their bodies were hot to touch.*
>
> — Thomas J. Headlee & Robert C. Burdette,
> *Some Facts Relative to the Effect of High Frequency*
> *Radio Waves on Insect Activity* (1929)

What of that star-foiled moth suspended in the heart,
    capped in its tubule of glass and beating, ceaseless,
at the pit of you? The homely salt-footed corpse
    of Archimedes, cankered on a distant beach?
Pulsars sing the Syracusan fleet transfigured,
    all-tethering round, to an underhanded light:
waves that panic the white insect. Let us be cruel
    as each is wont, hooking eyefuls of God. Let us
be awed, hot-bodied in the immaculate shear
    of it—transfixed as if on the beam of a spear.

3

Populus deltoides monolifera

Plains Cottonwood

Populus deltoides monolifera

> ...a tree among the billowing waves of green
> became as a sail on the sea, a harbinger
> of hope and contact with the infinite spaces.
>
> — I. D. Graham, *The Cottonwood* (1931)

Hackberry

Celtis occidentalis [1]

By the sun-sobering reach of him, King Catkin
gestures up a universe of shade and worry;
berries, summer-plump, ruddy in their retinues
and ripen on it. We underlings titter, fret.
For the flight of him in whom this passerine whim
has lighted, set its glassy flame, and rattled gold
from out the mellow-mastered stories of his rise—
how fickle-fleshed and minded of that southern clime
he conjures, green of mood, that lies like a heaven
and sure in the neverslant of sweltering days—
for such a flight from the last lay of greenspeech on
should wreck this whole and dark-depending world to sleep.

---

[1] *The common hackberry represents one of many shade-tolerant riparian trees associated with cottonwood stands. A so-called pioneer tree, the plains cottonwood by virtue of its exceptionally rapid growth and brief lifespan (c. 100-150 years) is often the first tree species to colonize suitable creekside habitat; once estab-lished, cottonwood stands provide shade for smaller tree species, most commonly willows, as well as food and shelter for a veritable host of insects and animals. Cottonwoods of both sexes produce, respectively, pistillate and staminate flowers called catkins. Seed dispersal, in which female trees swarm the air with silk-haired seeds resembling cotton, occurs on the Front Range of Colorado in June.*

Blue Grosbeak

Passerina caerulea [2]

Bayspeckle greening, strangers in the brood.   — *Molothrus ater*

By these I'd wager old Catkin's no king—

no more than place (mere place) be said to reign

time's sprawl, rooting; the season's tropic aches.

    I raise them. No—Catkin's axis, access,

    a fulcrum up from fleshly lives of want

    and gut-worship: a crippling of insects

    to the wild interregnum of the air.

Colorado River Tree Lizard

Urosaurus ornatus symmetricus

Sunny-blooded skitters | with gemmy skin and flits

to the boughnave swirling as days drip an ornament

on the land can Catkin be but seasprit whispering

---

[2] *The plains cottonwood furnishes habitat for many bird species, among which the Blue Grosbeak is a single representative. While the Blue Grosbeak's breeding range extends into Colorado, the species, migratory by nature, tends to winter in southern Mexico, Central America, and the Caribbean. Blue Grosbeak nests are frequently infiltrated by the brown-headed cowbird (molothrus ater), another passerine which employs a reproductive strategy called brood parasitism—depositing eggs into the nests of host species, on which the cowbird is utterly dependent for rearing its young.*

Raccoon

Procyon lotor

Toothpick moon in a grocery sack, nightscapes
    spittling up their daze of blue sparks.
The porchlight's rheumy eye is winking shut.
    Sun-sick, up from the cradlebark
of Catkin Hollow, I took to the creek
    and polished my fingers, shucking
crayfish. A trashcan's rattling, wind-walloped,   *— Faxonius rusticus*
    over and rolls out. A ruckus.
In garbage strewn to farther streets, the crows   *— Corvus brachyrhynchos*
    delight by day, and I by night
with greater relish and gentility—
    handsome feasts with city windows
honeycombed to a cellophane blond. Eyes
    aflint in the rotlight. Kits trill,
purr and whimper. There's a dream of concrete,
    a pit in the stomach, a will
that all creation's nibbling the fringe of.

---

[3] *Orthopterids—an order of insects including grasshoppers, locusts, and crickets—like melanoplus bivittatus commonly feed on twigs, leaves, and young shoots of poplar, a genus of tree species including the cottonwood. In the midst of an outbreak (grasshopper populations tend to balloon cyclically at intervals of 10-15 years), swarms are often controlled with microbial and fungal insecticides to stem rangeland defoliation. As with many insect species, the imago (i.e., the adult developmental stage) of melanoplus bivittatus does not survive hard frosts.*

Two-Striped Grasshopper

Melanoplus bivittatus [3]

Valley of Junestars. Many worlds.

Cold comes, unCatkinning. Needs fast,

too, and eats. Sun's tongue in the forb.

Wings fan tacky; windsprints. Grounded.

Green goes the one world 'til it's not.

— Helianthus spp.

Greenback Cutthroat Trout

Oncorhynchus clarkii stomias [4]

Was CTKN hatched the rippling terraces

    of breathless space and divvied sun

        from sun to pockshine shone.

Was CTKN bled and dressed in bygone days

    the tendencies of rain, kettling

        streams by knit and pillar.

Was CTKN flocked to roosting every ghost

    amid the green and leaf-lit scars

        of heaven and healed them.

Was CTKN barred and catechized us, split

    the blue above from blues below—

        the days you are glad in.

---

[4] *Because of rapid population decline in the late nineteenth century, decades before government monitoring of threatened species made data on the organism's range and life history available, the native range of the greenback cutthroat trout is not definitely known. The trout's threatened status derives in part from the introduction of non-native game fish (and the coincident increase in interspecific competition for food and in communication of exotic diseases), as well as pollution and habitat loss. Small populations continue to thrive in the upper reaches of the South Platte drainage, where this subspecies is supposed to have originated and where cottonwoods bloom abundantly each spring.*

Poplar Canker

Cytospora chrysosperma [5]

The cosmos bottoms on its Hadean vintage,

    vinedressers at the billion-lanterned break

of winter, whose cold in savage orbits slows them.

    By sally of the hatchet did his wound,

fruit-bearing, valley out onto a grandeur: meat,

    drink. Was Catkin cultivared and ringing

of Orion's bow, lesioned at each pluck and crush—

    understruct, salvo of the astral press.

Great because small because small because great can be

    but starlight stoppered in the organelle.

At the vintner's hand only un-enradianced,

    shall Catkin slough his season, king to cup.

---

[5] *While* cytospora chrysosperma *(the anamorph, i.e., asexual reproductive stage of the poplar-canker fungus) commonly occupies a saprophytic niche, proliferating on dead bark and facilitating the decomposition of trees, it can also exhibit parasitism in susceptible species weakened by environmental factors including drought, extreme temperature, fires, frost as well as sunscald, insect, or mechanical injury. Poplar canker infections often begin at the site of wounds. The disease produces black circular or ovoid lesions, which grow slowly in winter months, wasting host trees branch by branch as lesions eventually girdle and kill them.*

48

Chrysemys picta bellii

Deermouse

Peromyscus maniculatus [6]

Planks its rot-heart elegy out, the railcar's ghost—
    spoke to board, breaknecking a new moon down

from its haunt in the radio; pop songs Dopplered,
    boxelder riffling like a gingham dress   *— Acer negundo*

low in the luminous fishtail of midnight cars,
    curtsied to their simultaneity:

past, passage. The thousand pertinacious minnows   *— Hybognathus placitus*
    of bygone time still nibbling, hard as luck

and glintlessly, out where the garden was, or is,
    doggerel skulking in a feral rose,   *— Rosa arkansana*

dry rot unshingling the derelicts in their slump—   *— Serpula lacrymans*
    homestead like a foundered schooner, hull-up

and gutless. A dysplasia turns in the fine grain
    of everything. That pioneer wind's nigh

good as dead, Victoria, piano's gap-toothed,
    choked to the hammers with bunchgrass and sweet   *— Bouteloua* spp.

for dreaming of a woman's hands. Behind the dream,
    deermice like a fevered mind are spooling,

spooling up weedy lives, entrails of the dreamer,
    to nest their pink-bellied pups. How they weave,

bob, as if on a reservoir of vital blood,
    its through-rail and dark-harboring progress.

---

[6] *Notwithstanding its apparent ecological success, surpassing all mammals (even the ubiquitous human being) in abundance and distribution on the North American continent, the deermouse is widely reviled as a noxious pest. Its infestation of abandoned structures yearly gives rise to rural cases of Sin Nombre orthohantavirus (the adverse pulmonary effects of which account for mortality rates of approximately 35% in infected persons) and thus to zealous management efforts.*

Army Cutworm ("Miller") Moth

Euxoa auxiliaris

It's licking up the southern wind, moon-soothed;

a mothwing circus peels in blips and loops,

flaking the night's florescent eyes over.

Swollen on cheatgrass, greedy and glass-lit,   *— Bromus tectorum*

it's picking, parceling in at the seams,

all thump and flutter: spectacles of dust

loosed at the lampshade. You hear them fumbling

even in the utter dark, unstarry

but for a bulb-bellied god in the mind,

master on the mountain of wild nectar

and manic music. Plaster. Plaster. Thrashed

glass and plaster. The numb, half-pitied thing

crumples in a soap dish. On papered wings,

like that, it's kicking up and packing off,

over the hogback with ten-thousand moons

like carousel lights, glittering and slack—

the night a plum-colored hunger between eyes.

Mule Deer

Odocoileus hemionus hemionus

With Earth asleep in its celluloid reel,
dawn cuts, netherizing—a scanline scrubbed,
lightform corniced up the western mountains.
Here, the artifacted image clears, no
ghost in the grease-print, no backscattered star.

This, the penitent's hour: mule deer circling
purgatorial in their assemblage,
thieves in the garden, nipping up tulips   *— Tulipa fosteriana*
and lipping birdseed from lanterns we'd staked
where the wind-raked wild graced us, or menaced—
out where the wide roads end. We kept fences.
We did not feed them with our hands.
                              We seemed
saints, Elect above such as these, crumpling
down the interstate, heap by gore-flecked heap.
I know no prayer save this to raise them.

A population study: (Bartmann et al. 1992)
                    their numbers,
by the seasons' meter, boom and dwindle;
they glut and starve, all movement in concert
with the character of the age.
                              For now,
I ask only where and whether she wakes,
this winter fawn slumped in a photograph,
on the other side of her frozen sleep
or into the green of worship-worthy gods.

Great Blue Heron

Ardea herodias [7]

Sheer of water's photic spell, glimmerskin
he's Lord of, under. How the sun-flocked fish
wait out the sabered grok of martyrdom,
turning, *Oh-to-be-chosen*, at his feet.
Admiring miser, he counts the coinage
down their flanks; silver-strewn, one iris winds
its golden gear. *To know the pluck and slug
of a gullet-pink Truth—fin the slippage
sweet through, ah, the acid black of Rapture.*

Postured for the hunt, set hieroglyphic
sedge-side—how young and incorruptible
he'd struck you, who glimpsed him through a screen
of cattails and gawked with sheepish pity   *— Typha latifolia/angustifolia*
on stickleback, bluegill pierced and guzzled   *— Culaea inconstans,*
at his afternoon leisure.   *Lepomis macrochirus*
                              By firelight,
even now, slouching in a mudbricked room,
two grey ladies at a game of Senet
gossip, dove-soft, into dusk, savoring
the cool ceramic of their play—the names
of lost gods, tossed like tealeaves on their tongues.

---

[7] *The game of Senet, a secular invention of Egypt's predynastic period (c. 3100-2686 BCE), involved two players' movement of respective sets of draughtsmen across a board composed of three rows and thirty squares. By the middle of the New Kingdom (c. 1550-1069 BCE), the structure of the game had taken on symbolic religious connotations, the passage of draughtsmen representing the voyage of the departed soul— borne on its deathly bark through the twelve regions of the netherworld.*

Blue-Green Algae

Microcystis aeruginosa

The Orchid Born of Hades blooms, balloons,
and the lake like a ruptured cell; death stench
stirs, cytoplasmic, in the breathless heat.

As rot-eyed fish wash out, leering shoreward
in the froth, a scientist stops and shrinks
at the crumbling water's underlit faze,

the fever-green country of it, tumbling
to blue abandons. Battered little souls
wash out and out. The algae purl their mouths

and knit hot sunlight into teeth. Coasts of
carrion-cost take up diagram shapes
in the mind, and our scientist, alone

on the beach, humming unselfconsciously—
she's numbering them: awed, unsubtle airs,
music in the account of anything.

Rainbow Trout

Oncorhynchus mykiss

For whose sake must you prism out the light
that flies about your flashing flank just so
and with something of that ostentation
befitting higher animals? For this,
they'll split you, poor thing, like a zippered purse:
O the gem-red slick   and limp swing of you
cordons and strings   the dark-dripping rubies
that filtered your blood   all quick and glisten
as each gaudy drop   mints its crimson coin
atop the water

Ute Lady's Tresses

Spiranthes diluvialis

I found, profaned no door of pagan make,
warden of the wildland, no forest door,
trunk-subtle, in a lichened jamb long graved
of city-splintered nympholepts, no hinge

swung out to sheer the tantalizing glimpse
of her, this fleshly ancient at her bath,
eye of numen sheen, each limb delicious,
bent, water's gloss and beading down her breast—

Lest a strange life prize no stranger trespass,
never more an oread to blossom,
cyclic, out of brushfire, river women
rotten in the deep grove, streamside stinking,

hideous fish are coupling with beetles,
flight of waspwrithe jacketing the carcass,
sweet, curvaceous Lady of the Peachleaf   — *Salix amygdaloides*
bowed, willowing a wash of bloodied hair—

Wild, I found but little wild left to ease
a passage through, no door but the white-leaved
commodious plank by which I've shattered
this world to a delirium of leaves.

Woodhouse's Toad

Anaxyrus woodhousii

What mud-fastened soul strange as the stone's in you flinched,
    skittish, at the tamp of my foot? I, too, have moved
among giants speaking in the star-scented eaves
    of the world—poised at that untraversable league

past which the mind's lapse, landscape's heave, by blade and root,
    volleys through a heaven of thunderous discourse,
emptied of import, closing on a peace so deep
    the stultifying dark of it once birthed our gods.

For I might have cherished, little toad, a stone's soul
    like yours. I, too, have loved as a stone loves that share
of life I take no part in: comb of the moraine
    and canyon's cut, the lung's articulation sure

beneath its structure. A field in Argentina
    sweetens December with strawberry air. The world,   *— Fragaria x ananassa*
as it's always been, is full. Not a thing shakes loose
    nor marshals up the grim, splenetic wit to drop

entirely out of it. Forgive me, little stone.
    I, too, have proved cartoonish—pressed like a daisy,
staling, dogeared in some child's book. And for all that,
    I'd prove never small nor flat enough to love you.

Short-Eared Owl

Asio flammeus

"Lamplight lost on the membranous casement,
midnight lapping—soft, osmotic—cat-eyed
at the pane; sickle moon, slick as pooled cream,
cobwebs spun like a needlepoint doily
and catching the spill of it. Throw that latch,

"won't you? Set a spell while the coyotes yuk,   *— Canis latrans lestes*
yuk it up, gleeful, on gore-scrap tatters
and humble kills. Gullyside, sprightly,
sylphs of the May wind finick wild lilac,   *— Syringa vulgaris*
tumbling idle-wise, sweet as a porch dream.

"Set still. Prick up your ear, won't you? Bard-beaked,
freckle-breasted, Brown Owl's out whoop-whooping
at the wood foot of the tamarack. Why,   *— Pinus contorta*
the vermin bunch their pretty whiskers, spooked—
Dead Creek bending to its own erasure.

"Old Cricket's picking at his mandolin,   *— Gryllus veletis*
plumb-tuckered, for the like of us, again:
stickler for struck strings singing out for love
of nothing in particular. Let him.
Hear? The milk-lit lawn's gone hushabye blue."

Sugar Beet

Beta vulgaris vulgaris [8]

Planetscape blanched to a chemical peel.
Furrow on furrow, tractor tread cracking
the flatland through to the weed-lipped progress
of Box Elder Creek, dribbling distantly,
a sound of human speech alive in it.

May and the green of my grandmother's grass,
a relief on the landscape. Her farmhouse
squat, hunkered like a wounded stag—vestige   *— Odocoileus virginianus*
of the Age of Asbestos, of turquoise
and television; an old radial
pitched on the garret, spoke-sharp and rusting
there, hung like a weird horn from the forehead
of the twentieth century, a fool.

The house, the stable in its ricket lean,
stands empty. Someone's curtained up the glass—
thistles in the window box, paint flaking   *— Cirsium canescens*
down her door. Grandmother's gone to her bliss:
how far, I wonder, from these people, hers,
whom she could not bear to love?
                              It's years since
we pilgrimed a box of my mother's ash
and chalked the rotten earth with turning it
here. I'd occasion then, asked, *what should rise*
at judgment, steeped in so much bitterness?

What should rise from the moon-fine dust, torn up
through some hole in the world, wry and blinking
to brush glyphosate crystal like dried salt
from the corners of its eyes?
                         What must rise?

By June, wrinkled leaves like so many hands
of beets will spring, gracious and fluttering
with inscrutable gesture, bulbs plumping
to bob, come harvest, in a sea of sweet.

This thing, this troubled marvel of our time
will rise a marvel, and sweetly anyhow.

---

[8] *The industrial manufacture of beet sugar, an innovation of German chemists in the late 18th century, was first established in France at the behest of Napoleon following the English continental blockade of the Napoleonic Wars—a maneuver precluding importation of cane sugar from the tropics to the nascent French empire. Alongside four imperial beet-sugar factories, Napoleon also chartered a number of technical schools for the training of beet farmers, factory workers, and mechanists. On the heels of the first profitable beet-sugar operation in North America (established in Alvarado, California toward the close of the 19th century), the sugar-beet industry gained a substantial foothold in the American West, where, by the middle of the 20th century, beet cultivation occupied even the meager resources of our family farm in Weld County, Colorado, where beets are still grown, season to season.*

Coyote

Canis latrans lestes

Obelus stung on the wind-scribbled dark, they hatch,

yipping and hallooing, throats pinked on a tether

of sky—cry, petty as kings, from the yucca steppe.   *— Yucca glauca*

Firs bow, shabby in the tonsured wood. Winter's stole *— Pseudotsuga menziesii*

glown moonless over everything. You read no grief,   *var. glauca*

no flint of jaundiced eye nor toothy slaver, no

landform salvaged of the polestar, no wittering

of sagebrush, witless, in the void beyond this room   *— Artemisia* spp.

where you're lying, steeped in the mistranslatable

nights of the pack—which bays now, brooding on that carcass

of the wonderstruck doe, roadside, its frozen seeps; *— Odocoileus h. hemionus*

(no) which keens over asphalt sprawls on the landshard;

which tongues (no) for the wink of a bile duct, pressing

the choleric fact of you. Make answer, O spleen.

Lend us your script, a Merovingian flourish—

make caytive the yowl, the frost-curlicued window.

Grey Garden Slug

Deroceras reticulatum

The bracing storm has ended like a life.
   A dissipated thing, slough of greyskin
hagging down the sky. Pallid, stalk-eyed souls
   have slithered, monstrous, up the rain-shod earth—
trails laid in viscid strings of filigree
   and whirligiging up the flagstones stacked
around your garden. Holes are opening.
   You can hear them, almost, in the squash patch:
the idle riddling of a broadleaved gourd,   *— Cucurbita moschata*
   of all that's green and good, mown anywhere
the slugs have slopped their snot-white forms, gnawing
   in the mirelight.
           A penance paid, perhaps,
to One behind these shags of cloud. How vile
   He must be, this Raintender; even you
can't stoop to palm the easy, lethal pinch
   of salt—for fear you should pollute your heart
with the shrivel of yet lowlier things.

Ergot/Western Wheatgrass

Claviceps purpurea /Pascopyrum smithii[9]

> *And he carried me away in the spirit to a great and high mountain,*
> *and shewed me that great city, the holy Jerusalem, descending out*
> *of heaven from God ... And the building of the wall of it was of jasper:*
> *and the city was of pure gold, like unto clear glass ... and there shall*
> *in no wise enter into it any thing that defileth...*
>
> — Revelation 21:10, 18, 27 (KJV)

A sewer's spuming out of Paradise,

all spit, spillage: lo, what Gold Cloacum

in the empyrean, squinting starlit,

pinched up in a height of black-belying

blue, hawks this jet of municipal filth?

Steppegrass founders in it,

   bluestem bunching   *— Andropogon gerardi*

 at the split-rail, dead rain perpetual

 down corrugated tin, and, drought-be-damned,

 the far field, too—mud puckering for thirst,

 April spurting eerie with thistlefires.   *— Cirsium* spp.

 The prairie leeches up a color cribbed

 of fallen things.

   For Jerusalem, raised

other than a spirework, living topaz

hewn by knack of the angelic gemsmith,

should fail with Earth-perpetuating yuck

to flood the wilderness. Beneath,

   June sky

 ferries the spirit in an endless hour

---

[9] *Ergot, a genus of quasi-parasitic fungus, colonizes a variety of grass species, including pascopyrum smithii—at last congealing into roughly grain-shaped sclerotia, a kind of mycelial nodule, on the spikelets (i.e., flowering heads) of its host. Once established, the fungus cultivates a dubiously mutualistic relationship with affected grasses: deterring consumption by herbivores via production of highly toxic and, in some cases, psychotropic alkaloids, while simultaneously coopting the host plant's nutrient resources. The prevalence of ergot tends to surge in grassland habitats after seasons of high rainfall.*

of tourmaline. Bloodrot ripens, kerneled
on the glume. How like idols in a drop
of dusklight tinseling their golden backs,
the cattle browse and lumber softly through,   — *Bos taurus*
clipping at clover and toadflax.   — *Dalea purpurea,*
                              Advent: *Linaria vulgaris*
a deep dendritic circuit's fizzling out.
Starry-sensed, its choir of needles, keening,
by rounds make maladornment of the dress—
        this flesh she's bred by, into, poor heifer,

        who bloats and drops, blight-buckled, to a stone
        sleep the vultures reckoned days since.   — *Cathartes aura*
                        Somewhere
on a torchlit street, St. Anthony's shade
discomfits the gangrenous man, who's slumped
at a redbrick parish wall, beckoning
the priest to consider his hand, what's left.
And look, Father takes it tenderly up,
turns it—this sinner's wage paid out, no doubt,
in blood; how they smolder, heaven-haunted,
the fingers, like scraps of tinder withered
with flame.

(cont.)

During the Middle Ages, ergotized rye and barley were often unwittingly ground into flour for bread, producing epidemic outbreaks of gangrenous ergotism in which many of those afflicted lost extremities to ischaemic necrosis—a result of vasoconstrictive compounds loosed from the ergot incorporated in their diets. Now largely a concern for livestock, ergotism plagued human populations even into the twentieth century. Symptoms begin with a tingling and then burning in the limbs, followed by an extinction of sensation and a blackening of the flesh. The Hospital Brothers of St. Anthony, whose namesake is thought to have perished miserably of gangrenous ergotism sometime in the 13th century, became renowned for treating the disease to occasional, ostensibly miraculous success. Before the advent of modern mycology, ergotism was known in Europe as the ignis sacer *or St. Anthony's fire.*

The city's lantern-lattice spits
its shadows, hatching down the byways, out.
Father starts.
        With charcoal sheen, the index
splits, suddenly, unseated at its knuckle—
O how utterly bloodless as it cracks
and flakes to settle like a paper ship,
sluggish on the streetside gutter, listing,

    and glides: destined past the village bulwark,
    even to those barley-stippled hills, where   *— Hordeum vulgare*
    tillers, hunched, mounting the star-hounded dawn,
    plod ruthlessly, glazed in auriferous light.

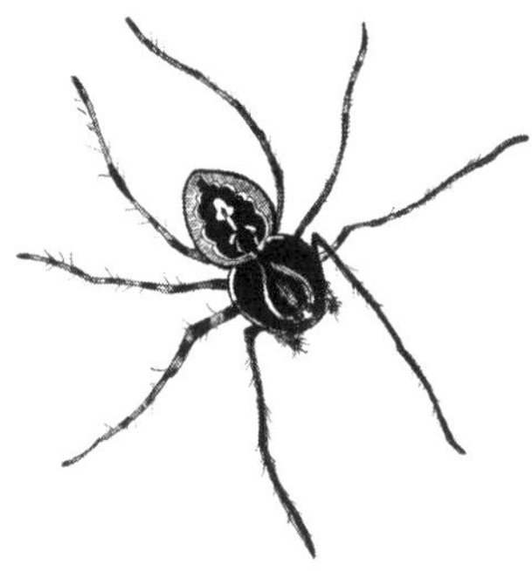

59

Larinioides sclopetarius

Indian Paintbrush

Castilleja linariifolia

Of a death in the house, revelation
paisleyed its curtains, floors—fade half-patterned
on the atmosphere. Spade in hand, father
tooled up earthworms, arrowheads. Strange pigments   *— Lumbricus terrestris*
bled through that ineluctable country

of air, uncertain for this century,
its hive-dwelling dead.
                     Blooms in the bunchgrass   *— Bouteloua* spp.
obsessing the bees. Quit, too, your bumbling   *— Anthidium* spp.
tongue from it. O necktar of forgetfulnesse...

Harvester Ant

Pogonomyrmex occidentalis [10]

Less the Toltec emperor, stepped to crown
his high, sun-civilizing monument,
limestone cut to shade with green serration
in the jungle trees, this drone, glob-bodied,
squat on an anthill's slouching pyramid,
lucent as a blood clot, sets his dull gaze,
black volcanic beadwork of its organ—
antennae tonguing some chemical braid
he takes up, dainty, off the wind's command.
A city-state bleeds in the subterrane,
switchgrass galactic in its spiral arms,   *— Panicum virgatum*
and, cast of slanting afternoon, he's still less,
how unutterably, damnably small.

Look—this sky, a feathered serpent sleeping,
coils on its blue frontiers. The past stays past.
Some lonesome boy on a backyard terrace
sets his gentle, barbarian laughter
scudding like a dugout on the Sagebrush Sea.   *— Artemisia* spp.

---

[10] *As a boy, confused by the oft-voiced anxieties of adults over ecological invaders, I mistook this native species for solenopsis invicta, a red South American fire ant with an increasing distribution across North America since its accidental introduction to Mobile, Alabama sometime between 1933 and 1945. The fire ant, reviled for its displacement of indigenous insect and vertebrate species (not to mention its painful sting) was then rivaled only, perhaps, by the Russian olive (elaeagnus angustifolia) as an object of communal hatred.*

Pronghorn

Antilocapra americana

I've perched me on the paling blue crescent
of a backyard swing, slack and dubious,
pill-capsule moon on its drop in the air.

By pitiless grist, the drought years clouding
at the scuff of my heel wind silt-spires, stirred
to an ekphrasis, pity, of water.

But sat on this swing, dandling the apple
of memory—reddish and rot-soft, poor
and euphoric in the pink of my hand—

I'm almost a boy, pointing: the prairie
since pieced away to houses, ricked with ribs
of timber, tacked up, so many matchsticks

bunched in the tinder grass. The antelope
in a shimmer of limbs are vanishing,
hoof by breeze-soft hoof, taking their places

at the outer spiral; the slow shades ring
hell's vestibule, one herd circling under
a home I've scarcely spit enough to hate.

Russian Olive

Elaeagnus angustifolia "

O wind-wizened ghost of the homestead, you
followed the tamarisk out from its brake   — *Tamarix pentandra*

in the garden, and, scattering silver
as you went, an accident of empire,

swallowed whole the fruitless plain—like Adam,
uncultivable. Powerless the axe

to stanch the spirit of your bleeding sap,
you rose, river-stitched at each blow, each crack

and toothmark. Many-headed revenant,
empty-headed golem of our misprise.

Deep with dowsing root, you drank the drought years
to their lees, battening the silt earth hard

against each dry and violent transport
of storm. O wastrel of the windbreak, we

hate but the error we carry by blood,
carry by blood, and carry by touch of

gold, touch of flame. We'd chrome the holy moon
to read our faces in it as we must

in all—embers unshackling the thornwood
up its progress, plume to black and skylong plume.

" *Following its introduction to the Western Territories in the late nineteenth century, the Russian olive prolif-
erated far beyond the ornamental gardens and country windbreaks in which early settlers planted it—an arc
largely paralleled in the ecological fate of the reviled and widespread saltcedar tamarisk, another riparian
tree. Even so, no other invasive species inspires the same animus among rural folk (perhaps by virtue of its
thorns, which hinder removal by hand), and efforts to cull the organism and blunt its spread have been histor-
ically vigorous, even vicious—to what avail, the landscape with its silver flocks betrays each year.*

Canada Goose

Branta canadensis

Whorl and quotient, bawling, cuts a torrent of heat
to the library door. Tables roused to flutter
with the brief and thousand-folding galvanism
of a life. The patron knocks his boot, snow crowding,
creased about his shoulders. December claps her maw
at the jamb.
        And for each open-blown page, a wing
turning, muffled on the darkness...where you've heard them,
cackling and bivouacked on the frozen lake, beached
beyond, such multitudes of geese as might tarry
or spring, ten thousand shrewd oarsmen mounting the air,
who row and divide, trailing their slackened hawsers
like lures to the very drift of thought.
        A log pops,
sheds its scaly embers, sparking, in the firegrate.
And the door's latched shut, papers slumped, sane and deathlike,
even as you've gone: a tin ship of consciousness
lost on the night, aliened as a straggling goose
and striving to follow what this storm devils out,
cloudlessly, upon a field of pointillist's stars—

somewhere on the prairie hearth that held your mother
holding you as she read once from a giant's book,
fifty Christmases since, and mark, her meaning clear,
even as all the world was pieced apart and drowned
in the cachinnations of winter birds, spun high
above your sleep, your home. Some place you've never been.

Rocky Mountain Capshell Snail

Acroloxus coloradensis [12]

I.

Nautilus lost on the Alps. Nostalgia

for the solenoid drummer, the clickshut

of Pleistocene horses, seafoam breaking.   *— Equus conversidens*

II.

Down. Yoke me the sick, unshimmering drive

of Elysian chariots; burn me,

fellowfeeling, for the trampled insect.

III.

Lodged in the soft, decrystalizing brain

of a glacier, St. Christopher's missing

them: knucklebones—rapt, stone-scarred in the melt.

---

[12] *The capshell snail, distinguished by its drab, conical shell, persists in relict populations, isolated among the Rocky Mountains of the American West and pocked likewise about the landscapes of eastern Canada. This curious distribution may be attributable to climatic changes that followed on Earth's transition from the last glacial maximum to a period of relative warm. Such populations as remain predominate in freezing mountain lakes and slow-running rivers.*

Quaking Aspen/Orange Cap Bolete

Populus tremuloides/Leccinum insigne[13]

She'd wet the tendrils of a foundling thirst
and pattern-knit each phantom synapse dimmed
to dirt, to darks of dreamless Mastodon,   *— Mammut americanum*
as, purling up the rot-swept sockets, she,
now eldest of a thousand sisters, split,
twinning out her virid tresses—past grief
grieving at the Pleistocene's mouth. The Age
of Winter wasted toward an ocean,
a black vastness after landscape, a drum.
A comely aspen wood meanwhile began.
Selfsame sprung sister, sister, and sister.
At each insistent rise,

    white-tongued fungus:

  fibrillose, broad-capped, dullish and gill-girt, — (10-15cm), convex to planoconvex
  wide stipe blushing like a wine-bruised carpet. — (2-2.5 cm at apex), clavate, solid
  Mars to Prout's brown in youth, velutinous;
  late life, pileus tawny to russet.
  Spores of like hue. Few to gregarious — amber, ochraceous in Melzer's reagent
  in litterfall, aspen trash. Mild to taste
  and tender-fleshed. Twining mycorrhizal; — read: ecto
  an easy, mutual thing—root music.

Down centuries of sisters, sweetly, she
struck fast and sang, the bubbling boletes come,
loosed of winter's anchorage, a-bob, both
born of water, blessed of rot—shriveled soon
to soulstuff, death-tethered specimens pruned
in a formaldehyde of borrowed words:

  old codes swimming yet the cell's soft cosmos

  for all the rainfall's sweet religion, gone.

She will go, too, the sisterhood in tow—

and I, with springtime and the mammoth, I

who rummaged for a touch of lasting life,

prized of her native continuity,

of the bone-quiet communion of things;

divined in the glass-eyed microscope, I,

who inked this offering—who tongued the skull

for sheltering thought, sciences for sake of faith.

— Mammuthus columbi

---

[13] *In the arid American West, where climate has remained hostile to the establishment of aspen seedlings since the last glaciation, aspens often propagate by suckering—a process by which new trees are generated asexually from a network of buried roots. Because an entire stand of aspen may comprise a single genetic individual, old stems perishing as new stems spring, the organism may enjoy a longevity of thousands of years. Aspen benefit from a host of mycorrhizal fungi species (among these, leccinum insigne). As the mycelium of an ectomycorrhizal fungus extends through the soil, it forms a mutualistic, extracellular association with the root systems of nearby trees, facilitating the trees' uptake of phosphorous and nitrogen while feeding on plant carbohydrates, which it converts to fungal sugars.*

50

Tyrannus verticalis

Powderhorn Cup Lichen

Cladonia coniocraea [14]

Our marriage gentles an aspen to dust.   — *Populus tremuloides*

With time, a mute distemper unnesting

the orbits of each year about the heart,

cellstarch and lignin, we—*we ungentle*

the elements moonside of this mountain.

We're kingdom and kingdom: *thine aspiring,*

nitrogenous, to gain the upper air,

lash the sea-green circles of our hunger

to a chariot star; and thine, to hold

another age the doors of Dis, dirt-fast

and creaking.

            Below, it's all machinespeak,

all firelight and charnel—weather systems

birthed of the prodigious dead.

            Traveler,

we tender out the crag-cupped chemistries

of toppled trees. We're not, as you've supposed,

the world's thousand supplicating fingers

flown to beg another name of you—*no,*

but a biding wolfnecked anger, hackles

of an order to outlast the city.

Fly thee, Adam, we offer you nothing.

---

[14] *Although naturalists classify lichens like any other organism under the Linnean taxonomic system, lichens are not organisms in the ordinary sense, but a symbiotic relationship between fungi and algae or cyanobacteria—a partnership so deep as to trouble the classical notion of species. In many lichens, the fungal partner metabolizes nutrients by its decomposition of organic matter and provides a structure for the photosynthesizing partner (or photobiont), while the latter fixes nitrogen from the atmosphere and generates photosynthetic products (i.e., oxygen and glucose) that benefit both organisms.* Cladonia coniocraea *is a so-called fruticose lichen, the medulla (or fungal filaments) of which grows to resemble bristles or spines.*

Tiger Muskie

Esox masquinongy x Esox Lucius [15]

Terms contrived, governing.
        "Tiger muskie."
State purchase. Sterile hybrid bred of pike
and true muskellunge. Child of estrangement
in nature; ghost in the ruck, ravening.
Hence,
    "Biocontrol." Thickets of fishbone,
flesh-set; arrangement as our appetites
by dint of law demand. Cull of trash fish
cropped for palate pleasers. Hence,
          "Assessment
of Environmental Impact." Prairie
as potential; landscape as a clay dish
deepened, dimpled print of the potter's thumb.

A trophic architecture.
      The stockpond
drops, shy of each administrator's draft,
to pearling verdure, duckweed to drought year
as benthic poor proliferate, fin-glint
in the undergreen. Lowlifes, spine enough
to shirk the plate.
      Up from Minnesota,
muskie by sucker and sunfish may turn
trout for the table, the loons unbloodied.†

— Esox Lucius,
Esox masquinongy

— Lemna minor

— Catostomus commersonii,
Lepomis cyanellus,
Oncorhynchus clarkii,
Gavia immer

---

[15] *Historically, tiger muskie have been introduced in lakes and other fisheries as a biocontrol to manage over-population of pest species and to free an ecological niche for game fish. Environmental assessments often champion the hybrid's sterility (instances of genetic backcross with northern pike being possible, but rare) and relative vigor as compared with either parent. Muskie can be reliably farmed and purchased for introduction by state agencies, though interstate transportation has at times been prohibited to prevent the spread of invasive pathogens—namely, piscine novirhabdovirus, which causes development of viral hemorrhagic septicemia in susceptible fish.*

As to funding.

           Any enterprise a question
of cost, consequence. Of prey compounding
in the gut. In all candor, let us ask
if the gain be goodly, if the loss be
ours to answer.

            Let us measure the brute
heft of it, set

           loose such slithering things,
sliplash of silver in the murk, master
by barren government—each to its hunger.

† Of some 1,250 esocid stomachs dissected at the agency, a loon chick has never been identified among gastric content.

Red-Tailed Hawk

Buteo jamaicensis calurus

The lisp of your lovesick shadow, breaking
its moment across the pavement, dissolves
at a black stroke, tabernacled in grass.

How, by the blinding circuits of your glide,
you wind the life-asseverating clock
buried deep among these hills. Trilobites

are twitching in the oil shale. A blowfly
clings to a hunk of meat. Out at the edge
of the buffalo grass, telephone poles

pin the patchless prairie to their patchwork,
tarred at its seams and buzzing hungrily.
Sallow down the asphalt, saltlights scatter.

But it's this heaven you're unequal to,
untethering the shades from their places—
and your own, like the point of a compass

curling, of a sudden one with the dusk.
You'll stoop, too, to a small and spiritless
view of things, the body's discomfitures,

retiring to some dark bower, alone,
to preen and pick the seconds underwing.

— Trilobita spp.

— Phormia regina

— Bouteloua dactyloides

Sagebrush

Artemisia spp.

By green of the deep-eyed breakers panting blustrous
    over Laramidia, hasp of shoalfingers
white upon the grasping rocks, a thunderhead burns.
    And it's thousand-membered, unmembering, the wind
falls to, unflocking the scrub oaks in their quaver—   *— Quercus gambelii*
    vermin swept to their earthen delves, and no cluster,
no seafarer's star to position the age, fired
    to tame billows of Indiangrass, waketrails strung   *— Sorghastrum nutans*
where the animals have gone. Even as this cloud,
    funneling its rueful element, makes landfall
have I pressed my nose to the glass—eye of false sight
    uprooting the splitrail; tangled anatomies
of wind and hill. And now that clock I'd buried grinds
    its mammoth teeth in ante-revolution, deep
below the cyclone, where pale things bide and beachrock
    is shouldering the promise of its spiral shells.
The sagebrush gutters up each dust-exhausted crest—
    tidewrack blown before me, fathomlessly after.

Common Milkweed Bug

Lygaeus kalmii [16]

> *Any large, strikingly colored insect, especially*
> *a common one, is apt to convey the impression*
> *"well studied."*
>
> — A.G. Wheeler, Jr.

Convoked of wings, O potsherd-patterned you,

who'd pluck the painted eyes of Attic gods

to sport them, hitching, wind-whisked up the creek

    any blink an Argus

           of black ceramic

shattered and recoupling (still, that giant

supped on meaner hills)

           For all your disco

danced botanic, dished of milkweed's moonlets,   *— Asclepias* spp.

you,

    mute subject, wishing the monarch stripped   *— Danaus plexippus*

from its chrysalis—westward-wicked on tongues

of tattling flame, no sinner's mouth begrimed

at the task of it

      how dun, unlovelied

on my predecessor's page   *See, e.g.,* (Borders & Lee-Mäder 2014)

        Pity I'd

missed you in my struggling contemplation

of the beautiful, trusting each to be

    defective if not

        kilned for other eyes

---

[16] *The milkweed bug's distinctive coloration—a clay-red 'X' converging where the forewings (otherwise grey) meet mid-thorax, beneath which close the membranous hindwings to join the halves of a bordered black ovoid pocked with a central (sometimes doubled, sometimes absent) white dot—serves a predominantly aposematic function. As an additional defensive measure, the insect is known to sequester cardenolides, a family of toxic chemicals found in the cream-colored sap of milkweeds, to thwart predation by birds and other vertebrates.*

Their diet but little studied, milkweed bugs have nonetheless been observed to feed on monarch butterfly pupae. Taxonomists (with a chorus of concerned gardeners) seldom fail to mention this fact—conspicuous in light of, if likely unrelated to, the monarch's recent population collapse.

Argus (often called 'Panoptes'), the hundred-eyed giant, appears in Ovid's Metamorphoses (I. 622-722) tasked by the goddess Juno with guarding Io from the lascivious Jove, who'd transformed the maiden into a handsome white heifer in a disappointed attempt to conceal his affair. After Argus is slain at Jove's behest, Juno takes up the giant's many eyes to set them forever in the iridescent feathers of the peacock.

False Parasol

Chlorophyllum molybdites [17]

Stain of the ethereal cup no king
since Æthelberht's drawn a bitter draught of,
toadstools fatten like figs in the forage,   *— Ficus carica*
an elfin ring at the tanglewood's brim.
Pared, pollarded to a diplomacy
of trees, the wild, fine-fruiting, is no more.
Light laps the orchard of a foreign Christ.

Up tumbleweed country, my heritage—   *— Salsola tragus* [17]
skulls of bison stacked in a parody   *— Bison bison*
of cultic awe—the prairie plaits her locks
with empty ceremony, wind waking
on the neck, yucca-pod stiff.   *— Yucca glauca*
                              Even here,
missionaries heard knocks in the dark, ache
of the old religion rankled, wraithlike
in the grass: rattlescrape of ós and ése.

Sprung dewside of one virgin hill no plow
could tame to cultivation—this of few,
half-fabled, to weather the oxen yoked   *— Bos taurus*
of the Homestead Acts—a fairy's circling
savagely, calling up her green-gilled shrooms
from an Otherworld isle without a name.

Hers proved a poison, steeped in spleen enough
by nineteen hundred, to open a door
in the backcountry and carry off the child.

---

[17] *Known also as green-spored lepiota and colloquially as vomitechristis one among a range of fungal species observed to sprout in so-called fairy rings. The organism's mycelium, of which its mushrooms are the fruiting body, consists of a buried mass of filaments called hyphae. As hyphae decompose organic matter in the soil, aboveground grasses grow lush and vigorously, enriched with nutrients loosed by the fungi's putrefactive work. This quasi-mutualism results in circles of dark green grass and occasionally, come rainfall, of pale mushroom caps. Fatal poisonings have historically occurred only in children and small animals.*

Ponderosa Pine

Pinus ponderosa scopulorum

Coppiced, stately, up from the Vale of Buffalo — *Bison bison*

(to which that scraggling ponderosan monarch worms

his clifftop down, six centuries of slakeless root

to crack the nether mountain, breaking on a glut

of cartridge smoke, plumed brushwise up, stale and grey-faced

as the shades, their mill of all-abundant wildlives

by stampede sound which teem the vault and plunging dim

of hell—summer of fireflies lost on its country: — *Photuris* spp.

sparks rifleshot, strewn; the light and then extinguished

blood; blood besotting there an unremorseful age

of pox and timber),

                    it rears in shaggy clusters

up, the forest, as if on tufted fetlocks, up,

herding its trunks by the sandstone anatomy

of hills like cocked shoulders, jilt and recoil, scarping

that exceptional wholly American blue

with which our sky looks on, counting them out *(the pines,*

all beetled through), seeming almost to appoint you—

                              — *Dendroctonus ponderosae*

none better to mind them, day's heat steep and pensive

where they crowd black-backed as a million buffalo.

---

[18] *Following its accidental introduction to South Dakota in a shipment of Russian flaxseed planted in 1873 or 1874, the tumbleweed established itself in a matter of decades as a prolific member of the High Plains' biotic community—to such success that it rose to notoriety as an icon of the American West.*

64

Ambystoma tigrinum mavortium

Black-Billed Magpie

Pica hudsonia

Tongues attuned to the carrion creature,
blood lumbering, and pitched at a ghost's gasp,
scavengers flocked along the living backs
of bison in their prairie concourse, picked   *— Bison bison*
and gored one crippled beast to a carpet
of glistering scabs.
                        Hunters, laying hands,
learned the damp and tack of their mistake, left
the knotted carcass for a chorusfeast
of cackling angels, fallen from the wide.   – Winter, 1809-1810

The Adversary, black-thirsting, himself
you'd eye by the whites of his wings—bygone.

        Fell the gilt spike of the Pacific Line,   – May, 1869, Promontory Point, Utah
        the animal of a phantom ocean
        threshing sagebrush clear to Sacramento.   *— Artemisia* spp.

Birds returned, rambunctious, city-scented   – 1977
from their vanishments.
                        Like a little king
the magpie trips and struts about his street,
stripping garbage, bore by bore, from a heap
of plastic sacks disgorging their shadow,
bovine-black, down a walk of foreign trees.

Would that one with his Easter glee should thrive
by what's left and prizing his savvy. O
would that one with a song like his should sing,
inheriting all the wasted world, and fast.   —

Black-Tailed Prairie Dog

Cynomys ludovicianus[19]

For every column of scalloped marble,
a void in the astonished ground.
                              Time was
the colony's black-fingered architects
sunk tunnels fit to dwarf the Roman dream

    of temples planted like a bitter wood,
    perch of the gilt eagle, high, petrific,
    fixed on pine-scented winds in the hillocks
    of Gaul—purple on her blowing banners,
    Latin on the tongue of every rustic.

Here extends a sea of midgrass crashing
up the craggy hogbacks: rain shadow thrown
leeward, Mare Nostrum *east to Kansas,*
Rocky Mountains looming like a ruin.

The City of Dirt seduced even birds,   *—Athene cunicularia,*
drifters fished from a wild blue, from perchless   *Peucaea cassinnii,*
haunts in some terrible yonder.   *Calamospiza melanocorys*
                              Time was
that reptiles nested there, skittering switch-   *—Sceloporus graciosus,*
tongued and sour-fanged—the gruff and gizzarded;   *Crotalus viridis*
packrats, rabbits curled, too, their soft bodies,   *—Neotama lepida,*
dozed the summer sun over from districts   *Lepus townsendii*
at the outskirts, noon sky shaggy with root.

    When the plague that cracked Byzantium   *—Yersinia pestis*
    squeezed its old corrupted lung and choked

her byways down with dead, our city rose,
bloat and blister, to flourish out the age.

Came then the homesteads, plows and braying beasts
of burden, sulfur and industry, men
    spitting their hard, barbarous syllables
    like seeds on the landscape. The good earth shook
    and shook for all they unplanted.

                      Time was
the college cooked up sixteen thousand quarts
of strychnine and cyanide on contract
with the nascent State, eight years campaigning
to tamp the ancient plain to pasture, cull
its teeming burrows to a catacomb.

The City of Dirt to dirt returned, spoiled—sacked
to a seascape silence belied by crops.

Two hundred miles off, across the mountains,
rainwater gullies, cool, down a quarry
in Yule Creek. In its throat of hewn marble,
somewhere amid the planes of angled stone
the rain now streaks and sheets and shines,

                      the earth
lies hollowed of a cornerstone block, raised
to lay foundation for the prairie church—
atop its white turret, a weathervane
swinging:

        aluminum rooster, throat to the wind.

---

[19] *Owing to the nature and extent to which its burrows modify plains habitats to the benefit of other organisms, ecologists have variously identified the black-tailed prairie dog as a keystone species. Prairie dog colonies alter the structure and composition of local flora and shelter a veritable menagerie of mammals, reptiles, and birds that make use of their subterranean structures. Because the local or global extinction of a keystone species threatens ecosystem collapse and the consequent extinction of associated species, some scientists advocate that organisms occupying such a role be subject to special public attention, legal protection, and conservation effort.*

Western Painted Turtle

Chrysemys picta bellii

In meeting, we perpetuate these lines:
I the road in its necrotic black, you
the blue, unbidden impulse of the cell
to scratch some shallow pondside grave and lay
the coming generation; slick of yolk
along the broodback, strung, the risen rise
to water worship.
                  With engines tumbling
in my ear, aloof, I should have crushed you
like a China plate and loathed the fragments
for my thoughtlessness. A mere, shattered thing
I'd make you, a tacky obsolescence
handed down from my grandfather's time. I
never knew him. For all this, I do brake.

And once I've laid you, my little Moses,
in the weeds, I pause—a tang of offal,
metallic funk of blood, boiling. Feedlot
up-breeze, the cattle moan. Perhaps a storm.   *— Bos taurus*
The future hangs here like a Great Red Spot.

Hoary Bat

Lasiurus cinereus

Jupiter's a blue electron, bubbling
gardenside of Paradise, globes of plum
in their pluralities, particle-stars
ajitter in the ornamental tree.   *— Prunus cerasifera*
Shivering, I drag the cherry pulsar
of my cigarette to bloom, to Doppler
distances—lone red point re-patterning
the animals.
              As Krakatoan ash
once unzodiacked the August eyelid   — Monday, Aug. 27, 1883
of the firmament and, burning, kissed it
'til an evening fell and could not rise, flaked
a mimic winter in its butterfly
descents—
              just so, O rag on dragon's wings,
you've journeyed to me, hissing cinder-white
in the aftershock of our acquaintance,
its brute intimacy among the leaves,
and now erupt, harbinger of nothing
but the night's celestial bark, buoyed
on a tradewind blown of tropic ruin,
by which you disappear—lone black planet
blinking panic through a wilderness of stars.

Western Kingbird

Tyrannus verticalis

Parochial as a moon, the ballpark's humming
with mouthfuls of silver. Late offices outlast
each planet popped in champagne percolation, clear
of Western stars and snow-lit peaks. A bottled dark,
blackshining, unbottles its gulf.
                    Above the crowds
and towers flecked with constellated lamps, some flash
of it, the dark, is darting out with fishly poise
among the halogens; a duskbird dives to pluck,
asplutter, at mayflies and dagger moths winging   *— Ephemerella inermis,*
(eyelets spent in the stadium's supernal blue),   *Arconicta americana*
then gulps with an air of decision.
                 A bat cracks.
The organist wakes from his August daze. Folk songs
and runners flown, dust up—not a body but thrives
by the light of cosmic sources.
                 Droll, the night pours
thick, vinaceously, along a bypass stolen
east of town. Freight trucks glare, momentary fossils.
Watch them. Duskbirds dip, feint, filching the daffodil   *— Narcissus* spp.
quirk of their bellies, brash, by turns through the highbeam
    as if to die
          by the bone-unsocketing grace
of God, and don't—
            but totter, endlessly intact
to swim some moon-polluted meadow past the city.

Greenspire Linden

Tilia cordata

Seastatic drones like a Monet lotus.
Cassiopeia bound in her night chair—
she's heeding that pale, insomniac blink
of the television;
                  stations close to
color bars.
          On him to whom the stone coast,
quavering by beam of dwarf stars bleeding
in a cathode ray, is many miles swept
as mere, sore-eyed reportage,
                a salt wind
breaks—
        limber fish unschooling the bloomburst,
invisibly, bulbs in the halide dark,
twitch of green from undercoin silver, blips
up the lakeside trees.
            He's angling alone
in the park, again.
             Wash of fleet-finned airs
whips irredeemable, tangling its tail
through the lindens, petalscent whiting, new—
new as any fossil might be reckoned.

Andromeda's distant. He thinks of her,
who died a decade later in the dream
he'll recollect, if only in outline.
Love left
       heaven like an onslaught in the lake.

—Nymphaea laydekeri rosea,
N. mexicana,
N. odorata sulphurea grandiflora

Rusty Crayfish

Faxonius rusticus[20]

Yrent of the Milanese glove and knucklewise cut
to downcreek scrabbling—bed of it sore and hovelled out
for love of industry. When a fisherman had sunk
his baited line, failing not to reckon the stonecleft
pulse of the continent's drift, Pangean, a crawdad
struggled loose of its barb; the waters teeming, spawnsown,
thrashed and muddied; and a mountain on its burning spine
had staggered then, brushed at grains of fiendish sleep, its eye
(redflame in the freckled schist and older than Milan
or even Rome) to set the North Pacific roiling—
islands cooked of the greying dust, bald, the salt air spoiled
with smoldering ejecta. What regna of glass, ash
unglistering the deeps. Treesprigs blooming in the slag.

Northern Crayfish

Faxonius virilis

Still, this river brooks the sere, tectonic ache,

any creature of a piece with it, and must.

A sea to split the world shall split it likewise,

native of a coming age, to etch the shale

with portraits of animals. There's no notion

speaks to home save the rib's arcature, paling,

strewn against some flesh-abrading crook of sand;

nor all the weight of light, history's mothwings

withering, panicked in the smoke and compass,

the lamp's diasporas—not a patch of it,

not so much as a blade of grass that owns you.

---

[20] *Human activity, both recreational and commercial, best explains the introduction of the rusty crayfish, a native of the Ohio River Basin, to Colorado watersheds in the twenty-first century. Faxonius rusticus has been widely exploited both as bait for freshwater fishing and more directly as a food source for people. Omnivorous by nature and tending in its dietary preference toward benthic invertebrates, aquatic plants, and decaying organic matter, the rusty crayfish ably outcompetes native crayfish species (e.g., Faxonius virilis) and has been observed to damage aquatic habitat by its disruption of existing foodwebs and by increases in the turbidity of still water coeval with its introduction. Government efforts to curb the continued anthropogenic spread of Faxonius rusticus and to extirpate non-native populations have met, perhaps unsurprisingly, with little success.*

Dandelion

Taraxacum officinale

By this my single, sidereal thought
blown upwind, elsewise, otherwhere, down,
deposing the old order of the hills
where yucca crack their brutish spines, bristling   *— Yucca glauca*
like princes—how dear Dandelion errs,
O profligate heart, how she disturbs me
by her deeds of progress. Sinks another
turgid root
          sows the road with golden eyes
turned and turned earth   turned and   star-stumped heaven
    spurned to monoculture
              Cry, *constellate!*
O breath-battered blowball
             O   innocent
wish   burning that
          all   the   world be
                none   but   hers

Urban Fox

Vulpes vulpes

Hapless as a blanket, you've piled the miracle
of your body, the mercurial tease of it,
tail and all, snuggled up to the crude salvation
of a snooze on the tennis court, where bleachers step,
bracing the noon, to proffer hours of hard relief—
shade to cool clay.

             A lawn slopes, Euclidean, down
from the duckpond, its ornament of foreign blooms,
to the heat-miraging street. Sprinklers and chain link
signal starry on the August air. A car crawls,
groaning, purrs like a hornet over paper comb.   *— Dolichovespula maculata*

What does it profit you, with your flame prostrated,
out like a candle—your complicity in this?
Our city breathes, unthinking, in that dream, the same
that's lost you, who scrunch your wolfish snout and laze, twitch.

    It's a tower in some farther town that holds us,
      all the yield and destination of the country,
      like so many Ducats, twinkling, in a ledger.

Listen. Cottonwood groves ghost under the pavement.
                     — Populus deltoides monolifera

    You've neither guile nor conscience, no glasscraft equal
      to a spire of such moment—deep, fluorescent rooms
      in which a lapdog curls, drools into his cushion.   *— Canis familiaris*
    Outside, a hard rain's ripping fledglings from the trees.

Cocklebur

Xanthium strumarium [21]

Shipwrecked in a briar of goat's head, your bicycle,   — *Tribulus terrestris*
its steel encumbrance, disenchants the afternoon.
Corralled, a roan colt whinnies. You strip cockleburs,   — *Equus ferus caballus*
prickling, from the shabby cuff of your pant, and grok
nothing—no twi-horned godlet winking in the pain—
but drag this whole moot enterprise of joy, boyhood,
a flotsam salvaged with your bicycle, to town.

---

[21] *The clinging bristles that comprise the cocklebur's chief morphological adaptation serve only the first stage of a unique reproductive strategy, promoting the distribution of seeds on the landscape. Catching on animal fur and cloth alike (well formed also to travel by water), the organism's ellipsoid burs contain two seeds, one of which germinates, typically, in the growing season that follows its production; the second can remain dormant up to half a decade, buried in the soil, to wait more favorable climatic conditions. Because of its toxicity to livestock, the cocklebur has been historically subject to concerted removal efforts. Its native range is not definitely known.*

Soapweed Yucca

Yucca glauca

Landscape lapses up the terraced garden,
stifling such arid rarities in bloom
as mother called from distant climes, tradeships
of iris and hyacinth—all the while   *— Iris germanica/sibirica,*
kneeling, prayer-poised. What she loved, she loved   *Hyacinthus orientalis*
like rain.
       The prairie whets its bayonets,
diademed of hostile force, a cosmos
glowing cold and hearthless;
              I am a child,
nursed of the nerve-white stars, once radiant
with pain as spine by spine my mother drew
cactus, *clumsy boy*, from trembling knee, *hold—*   *— Opuntia polyacantha*
with such staid grace I was ashamed to cry.

When she's gone, and the yucca up their stalks,
soldiering out a sailcloth of pale green
and native blossom, peopling the harbor
of recollection, they're—
             off to nowhere
but another of the mind's dim regions,
to feed on grief-deep fathoms of water.

Mallard

Anas platyrhynchos [22]

For A.G.

By the watchmaker's motive element

sprung to his afternoon preen, the drake tucks

as innards tick the green enameling

of that faultless, gem-bright head he carries,

bears up like a finery, prinking now

the fan-clasp fold of each ensapphired wing.

I've half-discerned his lost mechanic art,

the gear drive's twinkling teeth and symmetries

of weight and counterpoise, whirr of gilt chains

wheeling—the animal an invention

of Enlightenment clockshops—when it breaks,

this spell that's held me half an hour, dawdling

at the duckpond, where I conjure the dead—

yes, the never replicated genius

of Vaucanson, that

                also of a friend,

who worshipped with a sheepdog's heart, holding

that the soul takes no form out of nature

but the motion of its fleet machineries.

---

[22] *The once illustrious, now largely forgotten inventor Jacques de Vaucanson exhibited three automata at a Parisian exhibition in 1738—most famously, a clockwork duck which reproduced mechanically the essential anatomical functions of a living animal, including digestion, for which it was best known. Composed of more than four hundred moving parts, the machine's intricate design was never documented thoroughly enough to support a modern reconstruction. By the account of one witness, however, the duck appears to have survived at least into the nineteenth century—by then in a sadly degraded condition. His automata astonished Vaucanson's contemporaries; Voltaire compared the mechanist's accomplishment to that of Prometheus.*

Bridge Spider

Larinioides sclopetarius

Gnats bred to golden smoke, night-alchemizing, breed—   — *Mycetophilidae* spp.
    coinshine pebbling on the creek's bed; Dawn to brush sand,
      grain by mint grain, coy from the pinks of her eyefold.

A small hour enlarges itself. Truss-hung, lovely,
    the geometer, weaving, has shorn my spirit
      of its silver hair; for the plane of her window

in its high ecclesiastical shardwork gleams,
    taken only at a perfect slant. The footbridge
      groans as I shift, caught fast in these mesmeric silks—

where, frail as an eyeball, the orb weaver, feeding,
    shuttles creekflies to her awful mouth. A gravestone,   — *Chironomidae* spp.
      far and obelisked, dread-white as the martyred saints

      is stood: no figment on the landscape, no savor
      of the inmost place in you, that it does not see.

Rocky Mountain Elk

Cervus canadensis nelsoni

No tidewrack shanty from the drowned, no gull   *— Larus delawarensis*
nor humpback surfaced in its solar ache,   *— Megaptera novaeangliae*
love-stunned, loosed such a note of haunted bliss
as this lone bull's call—his herd by hundreds,
creekside, coursing into town; streetlamps doused
and dusk unblinkering the hawk-eyed saints
in crystal revolution. With Venus
first apparent in command, lesser stars,
wake-trailing, rise like the embrous blossom
of a knocked log.
                    They've come, camera-handed,
blinking from the low-lit bistro, this crowd
to whom such animal abundance stokes
awe with eager grief, fires for reunion.
Freed of heaven's sheepfold, such blessèd dead
among the elk by signs betray themselves:
consider the access tempting this man,
petition suffusing his slow step, stirred
by one with whom he'd parted on parched lips
and prayerless.
                    Hooffall drums downcanyon
on December turf, tires into darkness.
Some woodland beast makes answer to the first.

Herring Gull

Larus argentatus smithsonianus

The gutted carp, terrestrial anemones,   *— Cyprinus carpio,*
scavenged in their bloom atop the lake, lie rotting.   *Actiniaria* spp.

Gullflocks tatter, trashy on the overcast—blown
raving as if from some smoke-ravaged hive. They starve.

A rust sky reshuffles its forms, junkyard vans, depth-
desaturating. Slow ice shuts its creeping doors.

And the milk of afterlife's awash, disheyes set   *— Haliaeetus leucocephalus*
among these dead; an eagle, pricking, beaked with gore,

might stay the crows an hour, but you, you're too far out
to cherish each scale, opalescent, as he does,   *— Corvus brachyrhynchos*

the true reek of it. Coyotes, scenting by circles,   *— Canis latrans lestes*
deliver up the dusk—one Great Chain of Being,

bound and steadfast, there at the carrion center
with you, who watch them, rattled intelligibly.

For it's effortless as hunger the lone gull floats,
headful of paper. Mute passengers on the air.

63

Thamnophis sirtalis

Garter Snake

Thamnophis sirtalis

You've traveled, cool and mathematical,
up the earth's hibernal coil, scouring out
a patch of light to warm your sleeping blood.

What meticulous articulation
settled scales in the stonework of your head?
In passing, you're handsome as a statue,

capable almost of speech, if not guile
to slip the fatal lie by a black lash
of your tongue and unplenty the garden.

And yet, how speechlessly you scent the drift
of our mutual fear, of irises   *— Iris sibirica/germanica*
billowing like tattered ships at the rim

of an alien continent, and flit,
slick as sin where you disappear, dipping
down the terrace with its potted blossoms

and into the yawn of a cracked timber.
To what empty, bestial dreams you've dropped
in your world below the world, admitting

no command but that of my enchantment.
One hand's tensing at the throat of the earth,
where I cannot follow you to your peace.

Yellow-Barred Tiger Salamander

Ambystoma tigrinum mavortium [23]

> *...upon thy belly shalt thou go and dust*
> *shalt thou eat all the days of thy life.*
>
> — Genesis 3:14 (KJV)

The Serpent sloughed no bandy-leggèd child,

lopped of his smarting flank, but sank, coiling

dustward under the star-hard curse of God,

the canny sweep of His dismemberments.

From the carnage at Eve's ear, no creature

faltered its fatherless way from Eden,

ooze and black becoming, to scuttle off

for foreign fortunes, climates, continents:

the bud of jellied blood and liars' limbs.

And neither are you quite a golden soul,

drossed of the Refiner's fire, rarefied

with suffering, shot spinethrough and dazzled

with an afterworld magic.   What are you

doing here? Cramped in a limestone cradle,

rain-shone, where shoots of pinyon crowd the sun   *— Pinus edulis*

of this inimical century, ours—

all the soft things gone to rot, a droughtwind

flown over ossuary hills. And yet,

you live, improbable as any myth,

circling some mystery you'll keep from me.

---

[23] *In folkloric and philosophical traditions dating to at least the time of Aristotle, the salamander was supposed to be impervious to fire. While salamander species are capable of secreting poison through the skin, these animals' capacity to harm human beings was often exaggerated among pre-scientific peoples. According to one medieval proto-naturalist, when the salamander "slowly twines itself about a tree, all the fruits get infected with venom, and thus it kills the people who eat them." Clutching the trunk of a young apple tree, Satan appears as a salamander in Hugo Van der Goes' Vienna Diptych, a Northern Renaissance painting one panel of which depicts the garden of Eden. Astonishingly, nature has endued salamanders with the capacity to regenerate severed limbs.*

Colorado Hairstreak Butterfly/ Gambel Oak

Hypaurotis crysalus/Quercus gambelii

For these, the oak's luminous ministers,

one wants only a liturgical tongue

to utter some word for all the shining

things they are not like. *Crysalus*, ring of

crystal. Sting or gleam.

                    All that's glass-gleaned, carved

and star-swallowing, all science of flight,

the body's blink and windy oarage of,

yields us but little of violet-eyed Love:

> *for no male sought the lately killed female*   (Scott 1974)
>
> *whose plumbskin wings they blackened, hinge and pin,*
>
> *laid open like a book; they marked seven*   – Experiment 1. A(0); 23 min.
>
> *by evolution's libidinous pulse*
>
> *vying then to copulate with a scrap*
>
> *of purpled paper.*   – Experiment 2. A(7), AL(1);
>
>   2 hrs., 32 min.

                  Was blindness likewise

urged Milton, once, to couple the angels—

grand, pearlescent in the forewing's flake, but

holiest as stripped to principle, mere

in the alchemist's jargon: air and air,

the spirit mixed with its own element.

Godly in their desert poise, the scrub oaks

suffer the swarm its sap-keen pieties,

its summers of hunger.

                  Forgive us, Lord,

our gruesome love. Forgive us our knowledge.

> *(Dea cruenta, qui peccata scis*
>
> *omnia mundi, miserere nobis.)*

Mountain Plover

Charadrius montanus [24]

> *There has always been something strikingly columbine*
> *to me in the outward appearance of a plover's head—*
> *a similitude that is by no means shaken when we come*
> *to examine the prepared skull...*
>
> — R. W. Schufeldt, *Observations upon*
>   *the Osteology of Podasocys Montanus* (1883)

For I've parsed an archipelago of bones, plunged

to dredge the wreckage of a dove, unfeathered, up   *— Zenaida macroura*

from its acid sleep in the maceration jar.

Isle of femur. Of scapular curl. Isle of skull.

Landforms on a walnut table—and Huxley king

there, brooding over disarticulated ribs,

a scepter's heft, heel to the sagittal suture

piecing this world with the next. Borne from death's demesne,

I ferry morsels of creation's map: far more

of gore and gristle than I'd dreamt in the ghostbird,

seeming, as he does, aslink in his rangeland grass,   *— Bouteloua gracilis*

to traffic in afterlives—each step to glib step

a fluid vanishment. For all that wickering,

withal he's no pigeon from the Book of Tobit;

for I've seen, pierced to the white of his inner life,

yet never heard the call, and needn't. Huxley's God

skulks about those islets scattered through the study,

or else above. We've bone enough

                    to raise a ladder.

---

[24] *Thomas Henry Huxley, to whom the modern taxonomist owes an abiding debt of gratitude, was known among his contemporaries as "Darwin's bulldog," an epithet derived of his vociferous advocacy for the then nascent theory of evolution—namely his historic participation in a public debate with English bishop Samuel Wilberforce in 1860.*

Owing to its quick, fluent movements and its cryptic, grass-brown coloration, the Mountain Plover is known colloquially as the "prairie ghost."

Rocky Mountain Bighorn Sheep

Ovis canadensis canadensis [25]

Jupiter's scald, atom by aureate atom,
stealing first upon a ridge of Grecian tilework,
    dazzling the storm-spattered roofs like giant fishes   *— Mullus surmuletus*
with each bolt of His advent, stunned for an entry
    on the tallow-lit room where she sleeps, sweet coquette,
as if bored for the waiting and into that dream
    whereupon He spindles Himself, teasing at last,
drugged to a simmer with lavender, lanolin,
    back-flown about the immaculate thighs, burning,
gilt drops for love of her, the womb impluvium'd.

    Here, too, it's some ornery Outer god
    has spent the hairbrained vigor of his lust
    to turn the aspens, schooling and bright-scaled—   *— Populus tremuloides*
    mountain made sea of gold Octobers blown.
    The bighorns jaunt, particulate, cliffside
    of this landscape at their Perseid whim;
    they're smaller than you are, and handsomer,
    how charming in their brute conceit of it,
    contra Danaë, from the cragtop thrones
    where they buck and leer, theirs a dalliance
    of utter godlessness—joy and quick-limbed
    balking, heedless of praise, heedless of awe.

---

[25] *Following the revelation of a Delphic oracle that she should one day birth a parricide, Danaë, mother of Perseus, was imprisoned by her father, King Acrisius of Argos, in a tower of bronze. Seized by his famous lust, Zeus transformed himself into a rain of molten gold and visited Danaë through the tower's skylight, by which act the child Perseus was conceived, living to fulfill (albeit accidentally) the oracle's prophecy.*

Index of Species Identifications

Acer negundo – Boxelder ... 9

Acroloxus coloradensis – Rocky Mountain capshell snail ... 31

Actiniaria spp. – Sea anemone ... 61

Ambystoma tigrinum mavortium – Yellow-barred tiger salamander ... 65

Anas platyrhynchos – Mallard ... 58

Anaxyrus woodhousii – Woodhouse's toad ... 16

Andropogon gerardi – Big bluestem ... 22

Anthidium spp. – Carder bee ... 26

Antilocapra americana – Pronghorn antelope ... 28

Arconicta americana – Dagger moth ... 50

Ardea herodias – Great blue heron ... 12

Artemisia spp. – Sagebrush ... 20, 27, 39, 45

Asclepias spp. – Milkweed ... 40

Asio flammeus – Short-eared owl ... 17

Athene cunicularia – Burrowing owl ... 46

Beta vulgaris vulgaris – Sugar beet ... 18-19

Bison bison – American bison ... 42, 43, 45

Bos taurus – Ox ... 23, 42, 48

Bouteloua dactyloides – Buffalo grass ... 38

Bouteloua gracilis – Blue grama ... 66

Bouteloua spp. – Bunchgrass ... 9, 26

Branta canadensis – Canada Goose ... 30

Bromus tectorum – Cheatgrass ... 10

Buteo jamaicensis calurus – Red-tailed hawk ... 38

Calamospiza melanocorys – Lark bunting ... 46

Canis latrans lestes – Mountain coyote ... 17, 20, 61

Canis familiaris – Domestic dog ... 55

Castilleja linariifolia – Indian paintbrush ... 26

Cathartes aura – Turkey vulture ... 23

Catostomus commersonii – White sucker ... 36

Celtis occidentalis – Hackberry ... 3

Cervus canadensis nelsoni – Rocky Mountain elk ... 60

Chironomidae spp. – Midge ... 59

Chlorophyllum molybdites – False parasol ... 42

Chrysemys picta bellii – Western painted turtle ... 48

Cirsium canescens – Platte thistle ... 18

(cont.)

Cirsium spp. – Native thistles   22
Cladonia coniocraea – Powderhorn cup lichen   35
Claviceps purpurea – Ergot fungus   22-23
Charadrius montanus – Mountain plover   58
Corvus brachyrhynchos – American crow   5, 61
Crotalus viridis – Prairie rattlesnake   46
Cucurbita moschata – Butternut squash   21
Culaea inconstans – Brook stickleback   12
Cynomys ludovicianus – Black-tailed prairie dog   46
Cyprinus carpio – Eurasian carp   61
Cytospora chrysosperma – Poplar canker   7
Dalea purpurea – Purple prairie clover   23
Danaus plexippus – Monarch butterfly   33
Dendroctonus ponderosae – Mountain pine beetle   43
Deroceras reticulatum – Grey garden slug   21
Dolichovespula maculata – Bald-faced hornet   55
Elaeagnus angustifolia – Russian olive   27, 29
Ephemerella inermis – Mayfly   50
Esox Lucius – Northern pike   36
Esox masquinongy – Muskellunge   36
Esox masquinongy x Esox Lucius – Tiger muskie   36
Equus conversidens – Mexican horse   31
Equus ferus caballus – Domestic horse   56
Euxoa auxiliaris – Army cutworm (miller) moth   10
Faxonius rusticus – Rusty crayfish   5, 52-53
Faxonius virilis – Northern crayfish   53
Ficus carica – Common fig   42
Fragaria x ananassa – Garden strawberry   16
Gavia immer – Common loon   36
Gryllus veletis – Spring field cricket   17
Haliaeetus leucocephalus – Bald eagle   61
Helianthus spp. – Sunflower   6
Hordeum vulgare – Barley   24
Hyacinthus orientalis – Dutch hyacinth   57
Hybognathus placitus – Plains minnow   9
Hypaurotis crysalus – Colorado hairstreak butterfly   57
Iris sibirica – Siberian iris   57, 63
Iris germanica – Bearded iris   57, 63

Lasiurus cinereus – Hoary bat ... 49

Larinioides sclopetarius – Bridge spider ... 59

Larus argentatus smithsonianus – American herring gull ... 61

Larus delawarensis – Ring-billed gull ... 60

Leccinum insigne – Aspen orange cap bolete ... 32-33

Lemna minor – Common duckweed ... 36

Lepomis cyanellus – Green sunfish ... 36

Lepomis macrochirus – Bluegill ... 12

Lepus townsendii – White-tailed jackrabbit ... 46

Linaria vulgaris – Yellow toadflax ... 23

Lumbricus terrestris – Earthworm ... 26

Lygaeus kalmii – Common milkweed bug ... 40

Mammut americanum – American mastodon ... 32

Mammuthus columbi – Columbian mammoth ... 33

Megaptera novaeangliae – Humpback whale ... 60

Melanoplus bivittatus – Two-striped grasshopper ... 5

Microcystis aeruginosa – Blue-green algae ... 13

Molothrus ater – Brown-headed cowbird ... 4

Mullus surmuletus – Red mullet ... 67

Mycetophilidae spp. – Gnat ... 59

Narcissus spp. – Daffodil ... 50

Neotama lepida – Desert woodrat ... 46

Nymphaea laydekeri rosea – Hardy pink water lily ... 51

Nymphaea mexicana – Mexican water lily ... 51

Nymphaea odorata sulphurea grandiflora – Hardy yellow water lily ... 51

Odocoileus hemionus hemionus – Mule deer ... 11, 20

Odocoileus virginianus – White-tailed deer ... 18

Oncorhynchus clarkii – Cutthroat trout ... 36

Oncorhynchus clarkii stomias – Greenback cutthroat trout ... 6

Oncorhynchus mykiss – Rainbow trout ... 14

Opuntia polyacantha – Plains prickly pear ... 57

Ovis canadensis canadensis – Rocky Mountain bighorn sheep ... 67

Panicum virgatum – Shenandoah switchgrass ... 25

Pascopyrum smithii – Western wheatgrass ... 22-23

Passerina caerulea – Blue grosbeak ... 4

Peromyscus maniculatus – Deermouse ... 9

Peucaea cassinnii – Cassin's Sparrow ... 46

Phormia regina – Blowfly ... 38

(cont.)

Photuris spp. – Firefly (luminescent species) … 43

Pica hudsonia – Black-billed magpie … 45

Pieris rapae – Cabbage white butterfly … 1

Pinus contorta – Tamarack pine … 17

Pinus edulis – Pinyon pine … 64

Piscine novirhabdovirus – Hemorrhagic septicemia virus … 36

Pogonomyrmex occidentalis – Western harvester ant … 27

Populus deltoides monolifera – Plains cottonwood … 3, 55

Populus tremuloides – Quaking aspen … 32, 35, 67

Procyon lotor – Raccoon … 5

Prunus cerasifera – Cherry plum … 49

Pseudotsuga menziesii var. glauca – Rocky Mountain Douglas fir … 20

Quercus gambelii – Gambel oak … 39, 65

Rosa arkansana – Prairie rose … 9

Salsola tragus – Russian thistle, tumbleweed … 42

Sceloporus graciosus – Sagebrush lizard … 46

Serpula lacrymans – Dry rot fungus … 9

Sin Nombre orthohantavirus – Hantavirus … 9

Solenopsis invicta – Red imported fire ant … 27

Sorghastrum nutans – Indiangrass … 39

Spiranthes diluvialis – Ute lady's tresses … 15

Syringa vulgaris – Common lilac … 17

Tamarix pentandra – Salt-cedar tamarisk … 29

Taraxacum officinale – Dandelion … 54

Thamnophis sirtalis – Garter snake … 63

Tilia cordata – Greenspire linden … 51

Tribulus terrestris – Goat's head thorn … 56

Trilobita spp. – Trilobite … 38

Tulipa fosteriana – Tulip … 11

Typha latifolia – Common cattail … 12

Typha angustifolia – Narrowleaf cattail … 12

Tyrannus verticalis – Western kingbird … 50

Urosaurus ornatus symmetricus – Colorado River tree lizard … 4

Vulpes vulpes – Red fox … 55

Xanthium strumarium – Common cocklebur … 56

Yersinia pestis – Bubonic plague bacterium … 46

Yucca glauca – Soapweed yucca … 20, 42, 54, 57

Zenaida macroura – Mourning dove … 66

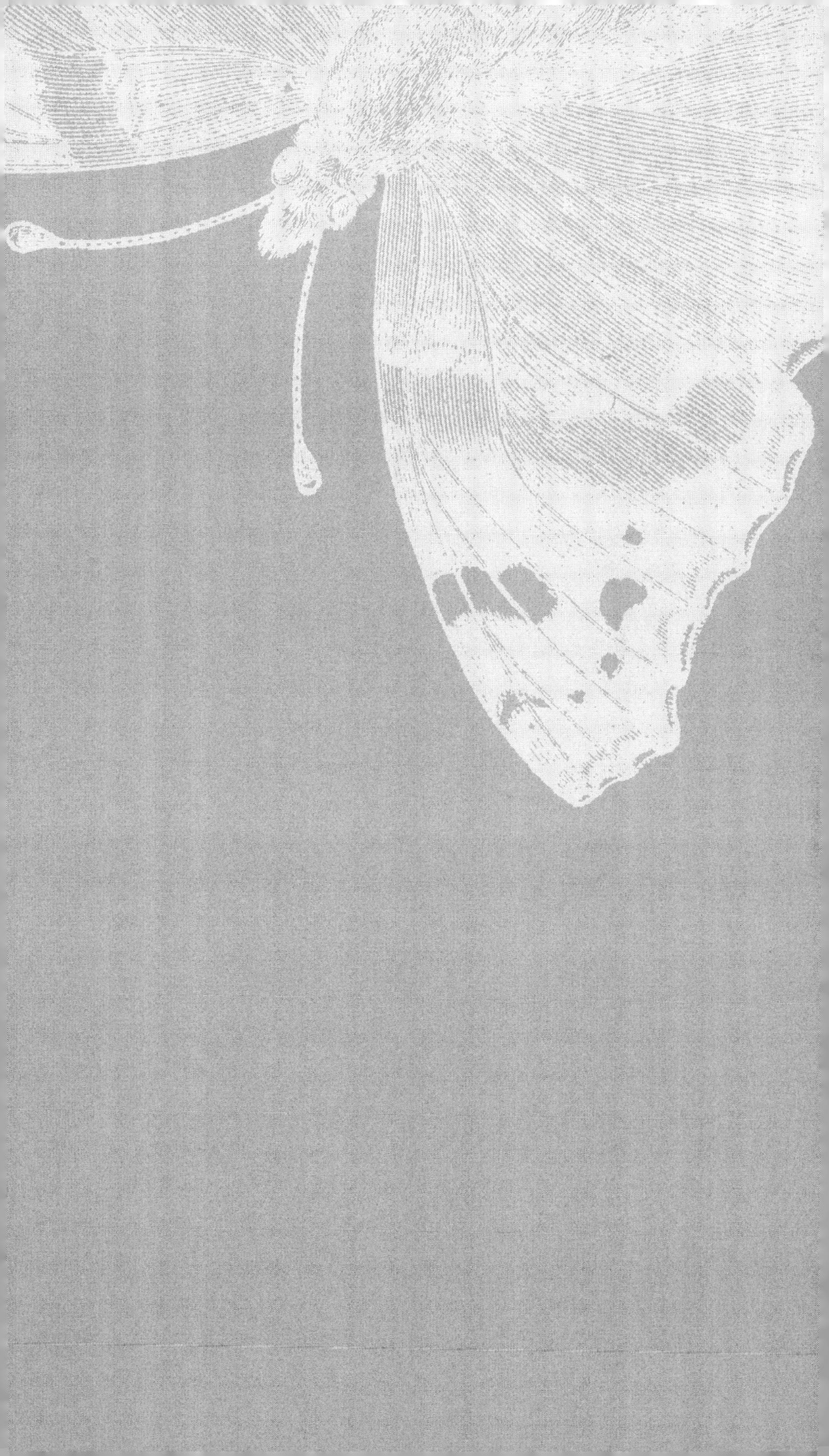

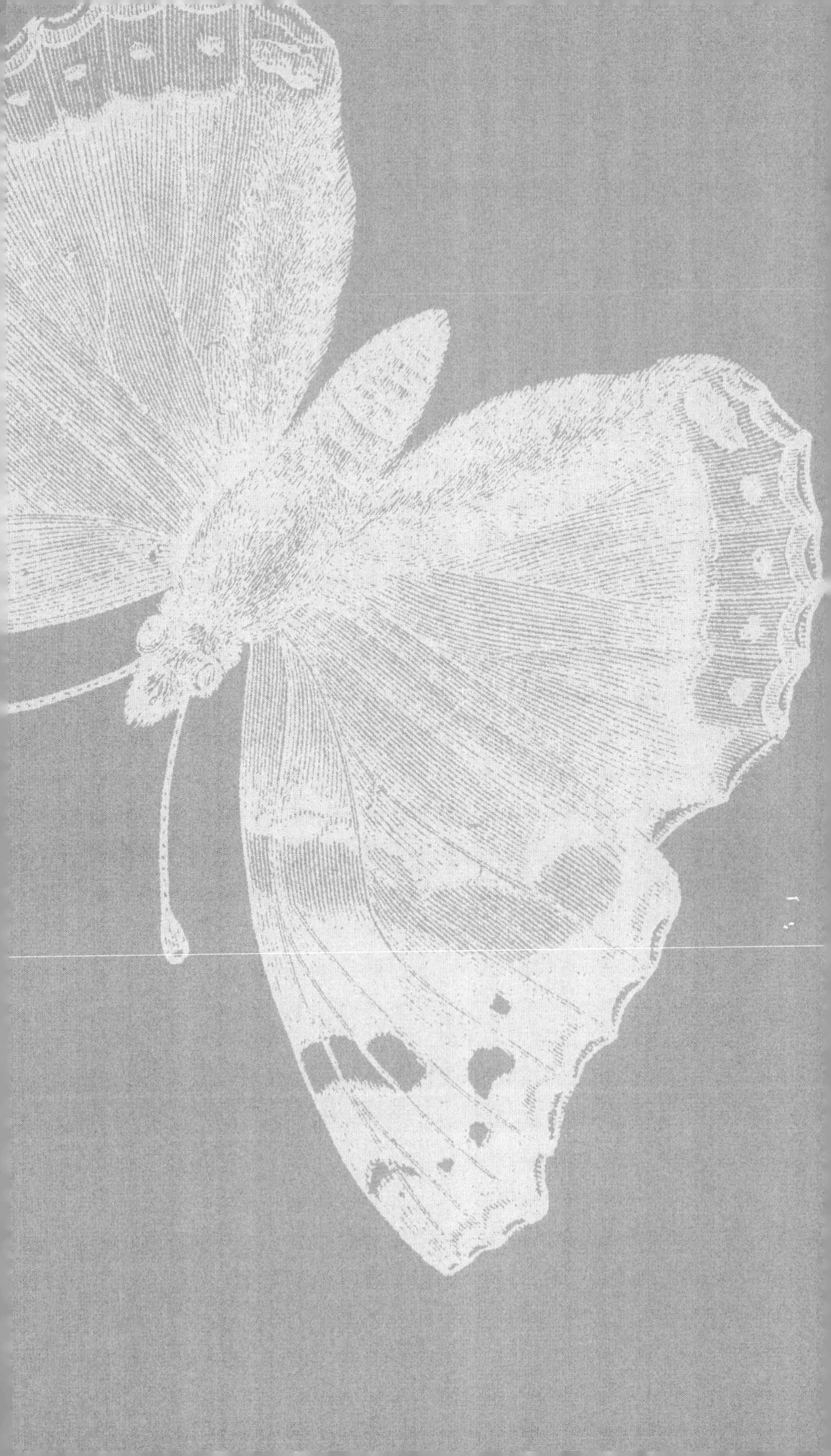

Bibliography

Agrawal, Anurag A. et al., "Toxic Cardenolides: Chemical Ecology and Coevolution of Specialized
Plant-Herbivore Interactions," *The New Phytologist* 194, no. 1 (April 2012): 41-42.

Anderson, Tamara, *Rocky Mountain Capshell Snail (Acroloxus coloradensis): A Technical Conservation
Assessment* (Lander, WY: USDA Forest Service, Rocky Mountain Region, 2005) 9-13.

Anolik, Ruth Bienstock, "Appropriating the Golem, Possessing the Dybbuk: Female Retellings of
Jewish Tales," *Modern Language Studies* 31, no. 2 (September 2001): 43.

Bartmann, Richard M. et al., "Compensatory Mortality in a Colorado Mule Deer Population,"
Wildlife Monographs, no. 121 (January 1992): 4.

Battaglia, Mike A. et al., "Changes in forest structure since 1860 in ponderosa pine dominated
forests in the Colorado and Wyoming Front Range, USA,"
Forest Ecology and Management 422, no. 1 (August 2018): 148.

Baugh, Albert C. and Thomas Cable, *A History of the English Language*
(Upper Saddle River, NJ: Pearson Education, Inc. 1935) 83-84.

Bean, Dan et al., "Status of Russian Olive Biological Control in North America,"
Ecological Restoration 26, no. 2 (June 2008): 105-06.

Beckmann, John, *A History of Inventions, Discoveries, and Origins Vol. II*
(London: George Bell & Sons, 1880) 136-37.

Beidleman, Richard G., "Unusual Occurrence of the Tiger Salamander in North-Central Colorado,"
Coepia 1954, no. 1 (February 1954): 60-61.

Beetle, Dorothy E. "Checklist of Recent Mollusca of Wyoming, USA," *The Great Basin
Naturalist* 49, no. 4 (October 1989): 637, 642.

Borders, Brianna and Eric Lee-Mäder, *Milkweeds: A Conservation Practitioner's Guide*
(Portland, OR: The Xerces Society for Invertebrate Conservation, 2014) 53-54.

Bottorff, Richard, "Cottonwood Habitat for Birds in Colorado,"
American Birds 28, no.6 (December 1974): 975-79.

Bowman, J.N., "Driving the Last Spike: At Promontory, 1869,"
California Historical Society Quarterly 36, no. 2 (June 1957): 103.

Brodo, Irwin M. et al, *Lichens of North America* (New Haven: Yale University Press, 2001) 3-5.

Brown, Bryan T., "Rates of Brood Parasitism by Brown-Headed Cowbirds on Riparian Passerines
in Arizona," *Journal of Field Ornithology* 65, no. 2 (May 1994): 164-66.

Bulfinch, Thomas, *Bulfinch's Mythology* (New York, NY: Dell Publishing Co., 1967) 93, 97.

Burgen, William F. et al., "Zoogeography of the Imported Fire Ants,"
Journal of the New York Entomological Society 82, no. 2 (June 1974): 113-114.

Chesnut, V.K., "Poisonous Properties of the Green-spored Lepiota,"
The Asa Gray Bulletin 8, no. 5 (October, 1900): 87, 89, 91.

Christensen, Clyde M., *Molds, Mushrooms, and Mycotoxins*
(Minneapolis, MN: University of Minnesota Press, 1975) 42-55.

Clark, Tim W. et al., "Prairie Dog Colony Attributes and Associated Vertebrate Species,"
The Great Basin Naturalist 42, no. 4 (December 1982): 577-78.

Colorado Parks and Wildlife, "Top Invasive Concerns: Rusty Crayfish," *Invasive Species*, accessed
December 29, 2022, https://cpw.state.co.us/aboutus/Pages/ISP-Rusty-Crayfish.aspx

Cranshaw, Whitney et al., *Insects that Feed on Colorado Trees and Shrubs: Bulletin 506A*
(Fort Collins, CO: Colorado State University 1994) 39-40.

Cripps, Cathy L. et al., *The Essential Guide to Rocky Mountain Mushrooms by Habitat*
(Champaign: University of Illinois Press, 2016) 101-02.

(cont.)

Cripps, Cathy L., "Mycorrhizal Fungi of Aspen Forests: Natural Occurrence and Potential
    Applications," USDA Forest Service Proceedings RMRS-P-18 (2001): 285-86.

Culver, Denise R. et al., *Common Wetland Plants of Colorado's Western Slope: A Pocket Guide*
    (Fort Collins, CO: Colorado Natural Heritage Program, Colorado State University, 2018) 4, 23.

Everette, A. Lance et al., "Bat Use of a High-Plains Urban Wildlife Refuge,"
    Wildlife Society Bulletin 29, no. 3 (September 2001) 968, 970.

Getz, Lowell L., "Notes on the Ecology of Slugs: Arion cicumscriptus, Deroceras reticulatum,
    and D. laeve," *The American Midland Naturalist 61*, no. 2 (April 1959): 485-90.

Giavitto, Jean-Louis & Antoine Spicher, *Morphogenesis: Origins of Patterns and Shapes*
    (Berlin: Springer 2011) 1-2.

Graham, I.D., "The Cottonwood" in *Kansas Facts Vol. II* (Topeka, KS: Chas. P. Beebe, 1931) 129.

Groom, Gloria, "The Real Water Lilies of Giverny," Art Institute of Chicago, accessed April 22, 2022.
    https://www.artic.edu/articles/886/the-real-water-lilies-of-giverny

Hamilton, Edith, *Mythology: Timeless Tales of Gods and Heroes*
    (New York, NY: Grand Central Publishing, 2011) 197-99.

Harrison, Jon F. and Jennifer H. Fewell, "Thermal Effects on Feeding Behavior and Net Energy Intake
    in a Grasshopper Experiencing Large Diurnal Fluctuations in Body Temperature,"
    Physiological Zoology 68, no. 3 (May 1995): 453-471.

Headlee, Thomas J. and Robert C. Burdette,
    "Some Facts Relative to the Effect of High Frequency Radio Waves on Insect Activity,"
    Journal of the New York Entomological Society 37, no. 1 (March 1929): 60-61.

Henriksson, Elisabet and Barbro Simu, "Nitrogen Fixation by Lichens," *Oikos* 22, no. 1 (1971): 119-121.

Hogan, Tim, "A Floristic Survey of the Boulder Mountain Park,"
    Journal of the Botanical Research Institute of Texas 13, no. 1 (July 2019): 33.

Houston, C.S., "Changing Patterns of Corvidae on the Prairies,"
    Blue Jay 35, no. 3 (September 1977): 149-56.

Huckaby, Laurie Stroh et al., *Field Guide to Old Ponderosa Pines in the Colorado Front Range*
    (Fort Collins, CO: U.S. Department of Agriculture, Rocky Mountain Research Station, 2003) 1-11.

Integrated Pest Management, "Cytospora Canker of Poplars and Willows,"
    University of Illinois at Urbana-Champaign, accessed October 25, 2022.
    http://ipm.illinois.edu/diseases/series600/rpd661/index.html

Invasive Species Compendium, "Xanthium strumarium (common cocklebur),"
    Centre for Agriculture and Bioscience International, accessed August 26, 2022,
    https://www.cabi.org/isc/datasheet/56864

Johnson, Keith Leslie, "Darwin's Bulldog and Huxley's Ape,"
    Twentieth Century Literature 55, no. 4 (December 2009): 575.

Kieval, Hillel J., "Pursuing the Golem of Prague: Jewish Culture and the Invention of a Tradition,"
    Modern Judaism 17, no. 1 (February 1997): 3-4.

Koch, Robert A., "The Salamander in Van der Goes' Garden of Eden,"
    Journal of the and Courtauld Institutes 28 (1965).

Koerwitz, F.L. and K.P. Pruess, "Migratory Potential of the Army Cutworm,"
    Journal of the Kansas Entomological Society 37, no. 3 (July 1964): 234-35.

Larimer County Weed District, "Thistles of Colorado: Identification and Management Guide"
    (Fort Collins, CO: Larimer County Department of Natural Resources, 2011): 16.

Lemone, Margaret, "Kingbirds Catch Flies in Coors Field — And Without Mitts,"
    NCAR & UCAR News, National Center for Atmospheric Research.
    https://news.ucar.edu/2118/kingbirds-catch-flies-coors-field-and-without-mitts

Lewis, H. Carvill, "Volcanic Dust from Krakatoa,"
  Proceedings of the Academy of Natural Sciences of Philadelphia 36 (1884): 185-87.

Magnuson, Torsten A., "History of the Beet Sugar Industry in California,"
  Annual Publication of the Historical Society of Southern California 11, no. 1 (1918): 68-79.

McAlister, Neil H. and George Mora, "Notes and Events: The Dancing Pilgrims at Muelebeek,"
  Journal of the History of Medicine and Allied Sciences 32, no. 3 (July 1977): 317.

McCafferty W. P. et al., "Colorado Mayflies (Ephemeroptera): An Annotated Inventory,"
  The Southwestern Naturalist 38, no. 3 (September 1993): 265-66.

Medin, Dean E. and Allen E. Andersen, "Modeling the Dynamics of a Colorado Mule Deer Population,"
  Wildlife Monographs, no. 68 (July 1979).

Mills, L. Scott et al., "The Keystone-Species Concept in Ecology and Conservation,"
  BioScience 43, no. 4 (April 1993).

Mitton, Jeffry B. and Michael C. Grant, "Genetic Variation and the Natural History of Quaking Aspen,"
  BioScience 46, no. 1 (January 1996): 27.

National Park Service, "Looking for Lichens," United States Department of the Interior,
  accessed November 11, 2021, https://www.nps.gov/romo/learn/nature/looking_for_lichens.htm

Ogle, Daniel G. et al, *Plant guide for western wheatgrass (Pascopyrum smithii)*
  (Boise, ID: USDA-Natural Resources Conservation Service, 2009) 3.

Ovid, *Metamorphoses*, trans. A.D. Melville (Oxford: Oxford University Press, 2008) 19-22.

Piccione, Peter A., "In Search of the Meaning of Senet," *Archaeology* 33, no. 4 (July 1980): 55-56.

Quinn, James A., "Variability Among High Plains Populations of Panicum virgatum,"
  Bulletin of the Torrey Botanical Club 96, no. 1 (February 1969): 20.

Quinn, N. et al., *Deer Mouse: Integrated Pest Management for Home Gardeners and Landscape
  Professionals* (Davis, CA: University of California, Statewide Integrated Pest Management
  Program, 2012) 1-5.

Ray, James D. et al., "Avian Use of Black-Tailed Prairie Dog Colonies in Shortgrass Prairie,"
  Great Plains Research 25, no. 1 (June 2015): 75, 78.

Read, R.A., *Silvical Characteristics of Plains Cottonwood* (Fort Collins, CO: US Department of
  Agriculture, Forest Service, Rocky Mountain Forest and Range Experiment Station 1959) 6-7.

Salo, Cindy, "Land Lines: The Cheatgrass That Wasn't There," *Rangelands* 33, no. 3 (June 2011): 61.

Schaffer, Jill A. et al., The Effects of Management Practices on Grassland Birds—
  Rates of Brown-Headed Cowbird (*Molothrus ater*) Parasitism in Nests of North American Birds
  (Reston, VA: US Geological Survey) 1.

Scheffer, Theo H., "The Prairie-Dog Situation in Kansas,"
  Transactions of the Kansas Academy of Science 1, no. 23/24 (January 1911): 117.

Schorger, A.W., "Attack on Buffalo by the Magpie (Pica pica hudsonia),"
  The Wilson Bulletin 53, no. 1 (March 1941): 45.

Schorger, A.W., "Attack on Live Stock by the Magpie (Pica pica hudsonia),"
  The Auk 38, no. 2 (April 1921): 276-77.

Schufeldt, R. W., "Observations upon the Osteology of Podasocys Montanus,"
  Journal of Anatomy and Physiology 18, no. 5 (October 1883): 85-89.

Scott, James A., "The Interaction of Behavior, Population Biology, and Environment in
  Hypaurotis crysalus (Lepidoptera), *The American Midland Naturalist* 91, no. 2 (April 1974): 386.

Shambaugh, Angela, "Cyanobacteria and Human Health Concerns on Lake Champlain,"
  Vermont Journal of Environmental Law 17, no. 4 (April 2016): 516-18.

Shaw, Robert B., *Grasses of Colorado* (Boulder, CO: University Press of Colorado, 2008) 596-99.

(cont.)

Sipes, Sedonia D. et al., "Reproductive Biology of the Rare Orchid, Spiranthes diluvialis:
    Breeding System, Pollination, and Implications for Conservation,"
    Conservation Biology 9, no. 4 (August 1995): 930-31.

Speckmann, Wesley N., "Dissemination and Germination of Seeds,"
    Transactions of the Kansas Academy of Science 19, no. 1 (1903-04): 199.

Speed, Michael P. et al., "The Dual Benefits of Aposematism:
    Predator Avoidance and Enhanced Resource Collection," *Evolution* 64, no. 6 (June 2010): 1622-23.

Stelfox, John G., "Fairy Rings and Wildlife," *Journal of Range Management* 32, no. 6
    (November 1979): 478.

Stones, Robert S. and C. Lynn Hayward, "Natural History of the Desert Woodrat, Neotama lepida,"
    The American Midland Naturalist 80, no. 2 (October 1968): 458, 475-76.

Thiers, H.D., "California Boletes. IV. The Genus Leccinum," *Mycologia* 63, no. 2 (April 1971): 272-73.

Tignor, Robert L., *Egypt* (Princeton, NJ: Princeton University Press) 29-30.

U.S. Fish and Wildlife Service (Environmental Conservation Online System),
    "Greenback Cutthroat Trout (*Oncorhynchus clarkii stomias*)," accessed October 10, 2022,
    https://ecos.fws.gov/ecp/species/2775

U.S. Forest Service, "Lichen Biology," United States Department of Agriculture,
    accessed November 5, 2021,   https://www.fs.fed.us/wildflowers/beauty/lichens/biology.shtml

U.S. Geological Survey, *"Faxonius Rusticus,"* Nonindigenous Aquatic Species,
    accessed December 29, 2022,   https://nas.er.usgs.gov/queries/FactSheet.aspx?speciesID=214

Vashro, Jim and Gregory Brownsworth, *Tiger Muskie Introduction: Draft Environmental Assessment*
    (Helena, MT: Montana Department of Fish, Wildlife and Parks, 2005) 3-10.

Weis, Judith Shulman et al., "Species Difference in Limb Regeneration in Ambystoma,"
    Coepia 1970, no. 2 (June 1970): 383-84.

Wheeler, A.G., Jr., "The Small Milkweed Bug, Lygaues kalmia (Hemiptera: Lygaediae):
    Milkweed Specialist or Opportunist?"
    Journal of the New York Entomological Society 91, no. 1 (March 1983): 57-58.

White, T.H., *The Book of Beasts* (Garden City, NY: Dover Publications, 1984) 182-84.

Williams, E.M., "Fairy Rings," *The Plant World* 4, no. 11 (November 1901): 206-207.

Willis, Craig K. R. and R. Mark Brigham, "Physiological and Ecological Aspects of Roost Selection
    by Reproductive Female Hoary Bats (*Lasiurus cinereus*),"
    Journal of Mammalogy 86, no. 1 (2005): 86.

Wyoming Fish and Game Department, "Sheridan Region Angler Newsletter" (2013): 1, 3.

Zamor, Richard M. et al., "Rapid recovery of a fish assemblage following an ecosystem disruptive
    algal bloom," *Freshwater Science* 33, no. 2 (June 2014): 392, 395-97.

Acknowledgements

Heartfelt thanks to the editors of the following journals in which some
of these poems first appeared, some in earlier versions:

About Place Journal – "Quaking Aspen/Orange Cap Bolete," "Sugar Beet,"
and "Ergot/Western Wheatgrass"
Bristlecone – "Garter Snake," "False Parasol," "Mallard," and "Short-Eared Owl"
Cumberland River Review – "Grey Garden Slug"
Faultline – "Great Blue Heron"
Flint Hills Review – "Black-Tailed Prairie Dog," "Mule Deer,"
and "Red-Tailed Hawk"
Harpur Palate – "Coyote" and "Northern Crayfish"
Image – "Mountain Plover"
Rust & Moth – "Cabbage White Butterfly" and "Pronghorn"
Split Rock Review – "Rainbow Trout" and "Bridge Spider"
Tahoma Literary Review – "Woodhouse's Toad"
THINK – "Army Cutworm (Miller) Moth" and "Ute Lady's Tresses"

NATHAN MANLEY

is a poet, translator, and contracts attorney from Windsor, Colorado. He is
the author of two chapbooks, Numina Loci (Mighty Rogue Press, 2018) and
Ecology of the Afterlife (Split Rock Press, 2021). Recent poems and Latin
translations have appeared or are forthcoming in Tahoma Literary Review,
Spillway, Image, Portland Review, The Classical Outlook and others. His work
has been nominated for Best of the Net and a Pushcart Prize. When he's not
too consumed with government work or writing projects, he composes music
as a multi-instrumentalist. You can find his writing and instrumental music at
nathanmmanley.com

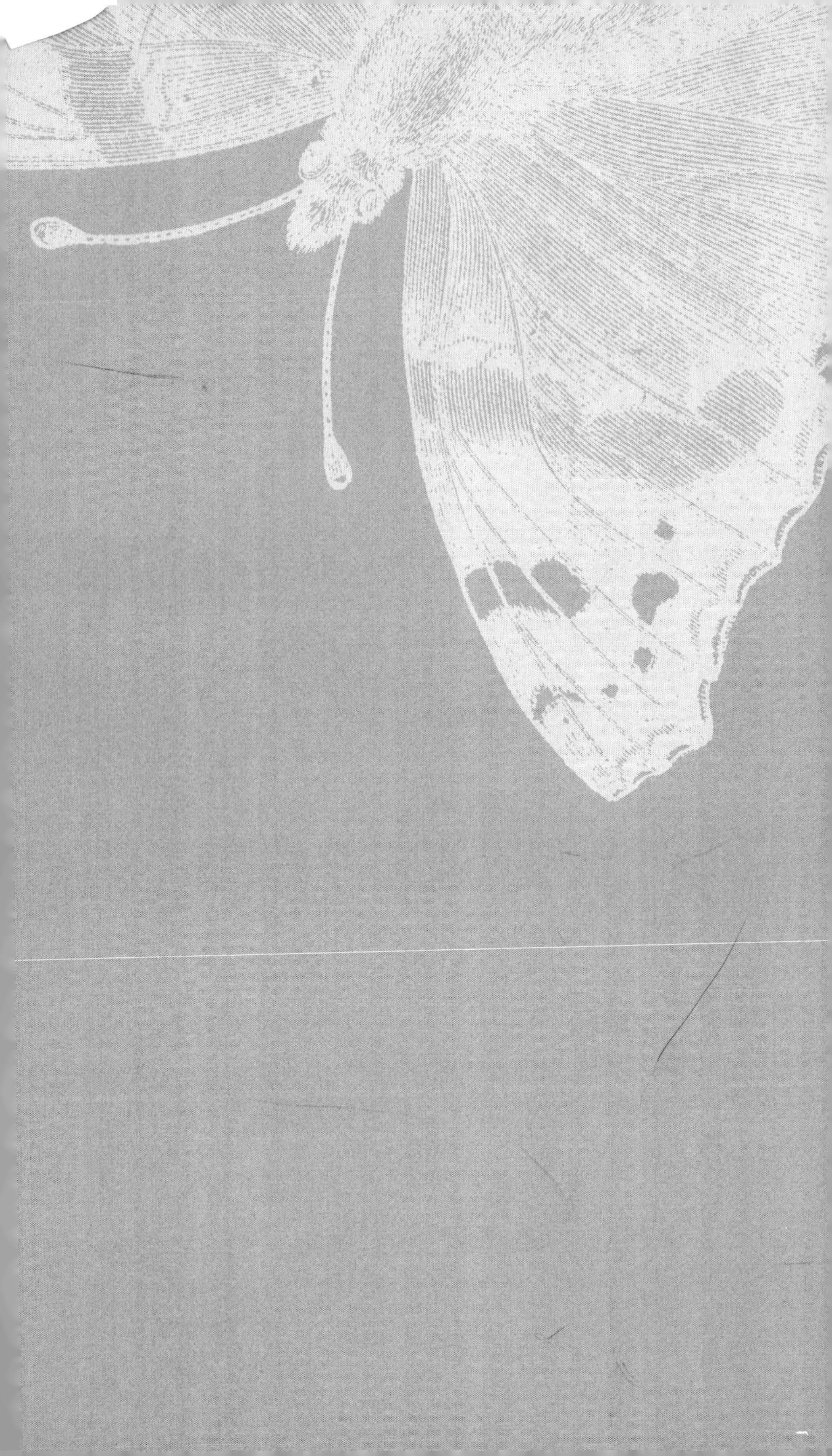